Table of Contents

Dedication Page

Dedicated to El Shaddai – The big breasted one: Mighty to nurture and supply

Copyright Statement

Disclaimer

The handbook serves exclusively educational and informational purposes. Both the author and publisher take full responsibility for accuracy, but they do not accept liability for mistakes or results from using this information. Users must consult cybersecurity professionals for specific operational technology problems.

Permissions

Request direct permissions from Chukwudi Abalogu/Logusman by emailing him at Chukwudi.abalogu@gmail.com

The copyright statement defends the author's intellectual property rights while educating users about their legal responsibilities and entitlements during handbook use.

Prologue

Organizations from different industries need to make Operational Technology (OT) security their main priority due to the fast pace of technological advancement and the expansion of digital networks. Operational Technology systems sustain essential operations in power generation, water treatment, manufacturing and transportation sectors requiring enhanced security measures. Cyber threats that become more complex and occur more frequently demand security protection systems to achieve extraordinary levels of system integrity.

"The OT Cybersecurity Audit Handbook: "Strategies for Success" provides organizations with comprehensive direction throughout the Operational Technology cybersecurity audit process to help them achieve understanding. This handbook supplies basic cybersecurity principles together with detailed approaches for vulnerability assessment and regulatory compliance that strengthen OT security systems.

This manual examines fundamental OT cybersecurity topics while highlighting the benefits of comprehensive audits through assessment techniques together with protective tools and technologies. The handbook uses real-world case studies to show how organizations implement audit findings and explain the necessary improvement processes for adapting to an evolving threat environment.

Achieving expertise in OT cybersecurity requires understanding that its challenges involve both technical fixes and cultural factors. Organizations achieve successful cybersecurity outcomes by developing comprehensive security awareness programs for their entire workforce. Organizations establish strong cybersecurity defenses by engaging stakeholders and promoting shared responsibility to protect critical infrastructure.

The manual delivers essential data along with necessary tools to enable readers to perform successful OT cybersecurity audits and develop practical improvement strategies. Organizations achieve valuable insights and adaptable recommendations for specific needs through teamwork between IT professionals OT engineers' compliance officers and senior management members.

The importance of OT cybersecurity will grow over time. Organizations have to establish sophisticated cybersecurity methods such as IT systems and OT systems merge alongside IoT device growth and the enforcement of more rigorous regulations. The handbook serves dual purposes as both operational guidance and an urgent appeal for organizations to incorporate OT system security into their business strategies while maintaining continuous improvement at the core of their strategic planning.

The following sections outline crucial cybersecurity audit strategies for OT systems and provide organizations with a comprehensive guide to protect essential infrastructure from emerging threats. We can develop a dependable OT system infrastructure through joint efforts to meet the requirements of our connected environment.

Chapter 1: Introduction to Operational Technology (OT) Cybersecurity

Overview of OT vs. IT

Protecting modern systems through effective cybersecurity strategies demands knowledge about both Operational Technology (OT) and Information Technology (IT).

What is Operational Technology (OT)?

Operational Technology employs a combination of software and hardware to ensure direct supervision and management of physical machines and industrial operations throughout various sectors. Operational technology includes industrial control systems (ICS), Supervisory Control and Data Acquisition (SCADA) systems and fundamental infrastructure components. Operational Technology (OT) enables direct supervision and management of physical systems which increases production efficiency and boosts operational performance in fields such as manufacturing energy generation transportation systems and utility services.

What is Information Technology (IT)?

Information Technology merges computing hardware and software with network systems and data management for information processing and storage. IT systems in organizations manage data and enable communication which assists organizational decision-making processes.

Key Differences Between OT and IT

Purpose:

Operational Technology (OT) manages physical machinery operations whereas Information Technology (IT) handles data management alongside information processing tasks.

Environment:

Operational Technology systems oversee settings that require prompt responses and rigorous safety rules including factories and power plants. IT environments are generally office-based or cloud-centric.

Architecture:

Operational Technology systems rely on static architectural designs to operate industrial processes while IT systems function through adaptable modular design structures.

Security Focus:

The IT security framework employs the CIA triad to secure data confidentiality and integrity while ensuring availability, but OT security ensures physical process safety and reliability along with availability.

Life Cycle:

Operational technology systems deliver extended functionality without requiring regular updates unlike information systems which demand consistent refreshments and replacements.

Entities need to develop cybersecurity frameworks that support both IT and OT systems through the assessment of their unique security requirements.

Importance of OT Cybersecurity

Organizations should establish OT cybersecurity as their top priority due to its ongoing critical importance. Organizations need to defend OT environments since cyber threats grow as more interconnected devices require IT and OT systems to collaborate.

Critical Infrastructure

Operational Technology systems enable power generation and water supply management while simultaneously supporting healthcare facilities and transportation networks. System breaches by attackers result in catastrophic consequences.

Safety Risks: Attackers who gain control over operational systems establish life-threatening conditions for individuals.

Operational Disruptions: Production line shutdowns resulting from cyber incidents lead to substantial financial losses and damage to corporate reputation.

Data Breaches: Attackers gain unauthorized access to operational technology systems in order to retrieve intellectual property and extract additional sensitive operational information.

Regulatory Compliance

Government agencies together with regulatory bodies require enhanced cybersecurity measures for operational technology systems to safeguard critical infrastructure. To prevent legal and financial repercussions organizations must follow the guidelines set by the NIST Cybersecurity Framework and the EU's NIS Directive alongside industry-specific guidelines.

Evolving Threat Landscape

Cyber threats to OT systems are evolving. Advanced persistent threats combined with ransomware attacks and malicious internal activities create significant operational continuity risks for organizations. The 2021 cyberattacks against Colonial Pipeline and JBS Foods exposed fundamental security flaws in operational technology measures. Recent security breaches demonstrate that organizations must immediately improve their cybersecurity defenses with comprehensive audits and evaluations.

Current Threat Landscape

Operational technology cybersecurity experts must always be alert to the relentless advancement of sophisticated threats that demand their ongoing focus. The adoption of connected technologies in organizations increases their attack surfaces thereby creating new security vulnerabilities.

Types of Threats

Malware and Ransomware:

Organizations face operational disruptions and force payments when malicious software encrypts their data.

Example: The WannaCry ransomware attack affected healthcare and manufacturing sectors by uncovering operational technology system security weaknesses during service disruptions.

Insider Threats:

Authorized individuals pose security threats when they unintentionally or deliberately create vulnerabilities in systems.

Example: Unauthorized software installation by employees creates security weaknesses in OT systems.

Advanced Persistent Threats (APTs):

State-sponsored cyberattacks execute extended operations which target both data theft and operation system disruptions.

Example: The disruption of Iranian nuclear facilities by the Stuxnet cyberattack showcased advanced cyber warfare capabilities.

Supply Chain Attacks:

Operational Technology systems become accessible to cybercriminals through their attacks on organizations' third-party vendors.

Example: Attackers used vulnerabilities in supply chain software updates to penetrate multiple organizations during the SolarWinds incident.

Emerging Threats

As technology advances it enables cybercriminals to develop increasingly complex attack strategies which are harder to defend against. Implementation of Internet of Things (IoT) technologies by organizations creates new security vulnerabilities within their operational technology systems. IoT devices present opportunities for attackers to exploit them because they lack proper security measures.

IoT Vulnerabilities:

IoT devices stay vulnerable to hacking because outdated defenses and weak systems allow attackers to exploit default passwords and old software along with inadequate encryption methods.

Example: In 2016 Mirai botnet executed a unique Distributed Denial of Service (DDoS) operation that exploited IoT device security flaws to disrupt major websites and online services.

Cloud Integration Risks:

Organizations that adopt cloud-based Operational Technology management systems face new security threats like data breaches and system misconfiguration risks.

Example: Data breaches struck multiple organizations because they set up their cloud storage systems incorrectly illustrating cloud deployment security risks.

Social Engineering Attacks:

Attackers use social engineering techniques to fool employees into disclosing sensitive information that provides unauthorized access to OT systems.

Example: Operational technology systems face unauthorized access through attackers who steal credentials from essential infrastructure personnel using phishing attacks.

The Need for Comprehensive Cybersecurity Measures

The significant functions of OT systems coupled with the changing threat environment require organizations to implement proactive cybersecurity measures. The achievement of full protection requires a comprehensive cybersecurity strategy to include multiple essential components.

Risk Assessment and Management:

Organizations must regularly perform risk assessments to identify system weaknesses and determine which actions need immediate attention. Organizations need to adopt this method to maintain readiness against evolving security threats.

Employee Training and Awareness:

Continuous employee training programs are essential to impart security best practices and OT system protection techniques. Employees need to understand social engineering tactics while learning why reporting suspicious activities is important.

Incident Response Planning:

Through the development and regular testing of an incident response plan organizations can respond more quickly and efficiently to cybersecurity incidents while reducing the extent of possible damage.

Regular Audits and Assessments:

Regular assessments of OT systems enable organizations to both discover system weaknesses and confirm their adherence to security standards.

Collaboration and Information Sharing:

Interorganizational partnerships and government cybersecurity collaborations enable organizations to bolster OT security with shared threat intelligence and best practices.

Conclusion

The challenges presented by operational technology integration with cybersecurity demand specialized expertise. Business operations that depend more heavily on operational technology systems must establish essential robust cybersecurity defenses.

An effective cybersecurity audit begins with distinguishing between OT and IT systems and recognizing OT systems' importance while understanding how threats change over time. Organizations that concentrate on OT cybersecurity protection preserve their assets and operational systems while adhering to growing regulatory standards.

This document examines OT cybersecurity audits in detail and presents both frameworks and tools to help organizations protect their operational technology environments. This learning journey delivers essential OT cybersecurity knowledge and practical insights while supporting the development of a security-focused organizational culture. Through our partnership we will achieve a more secure and robust operational technology environment.

The first chapter of "The OT Cybersecurity Audit Handbook: Strategies for Success" ends here. The upcoming sections analyze cybersecurity audit techniques and methods while elaborating on regulatory frameworks and best practices for safeguarding organizational OT systems against modern cyber threats.

Chapter 2: Understanding Cybersecurity Audits

Definition of a Cybersecurity Audit

A cybersecurity audit involves a thorough review of an organization's information systems, policies, and operations to determine how well its security controls work. A cybersecurity audit within Operational Technology (OT) examines the security status of OT systems while identifying system weaknesses and verifying adherence to standards and best practice protocols.

Key Components of Cybersecurity Audits

Scope: The audit needs to establish clear limits on what areas will undergo evaluation. OT system evaluations encompass hardware and software components, network systems and the surrounding physical environment.

Methodology: Multiple methods exist for evaluation, including qualitative assessments or quantitative measurements which can also be combined. Different methodologies possess unique advantages and disadvantages which should be considered when selecting the best approach based on the audit's intended objectives.

Assessment Tools: The audit process frequently incorporates various tools and frameworks such as risk assessment tools, vulnerability scanners, and compliance checklists which follow relevant regulations and industry standards.

Reporting: The final audit report documents findings alongside analysis and actionable recommendations. Stakeholders depend on this report for critical information which will direct future improvements in security measures.

Importance of Cybersecurity Audits

Cybersecurity audits fulfill multiple functions that support an organization's comprehensive security strategy.

Identifying Vulnerabilities: A primary audit objective is to reveal security weaknesses which cyber attackers might exploit. With this proactive stance organizations can resolve security weaknesses before attackers exploit them.

Ensuring Compliance: Specific cybersecurity practices must adhere to industry-specific regulations in many fields. Organizations use audits to verify regulatory compliance and avoid legal consequences.

Enhancing Security Posture: Audits promote the creation of more robust security protocols and incident response strategies by evaluating existing security measures and discovering areas that need enhancement.

Building Trust: An organization strengthens its standing with stakeholders, customers and partners through regular audits that show their dedication to cybersecurity and risk management.

Facilitating Continuous Improvement: Because cybersecurity evolves rapidly organizations need to perform regular audits to keep up with new threats and updated practices while adapting their security measures to meet emerging challenges.

Types of Cybersecurity Audits

Multiple classifications exist for cybersecurity audits which distinguish them by their specific focuses and methodologies. Determining the right audit approach for an organization's specific needs requires comprehensive understanding of these audit distinctions.

1. Compliance Audits

Definition: Compliance audits evaluate how well organizations follow applicable laws, regulations and industry standards pertaining to cybersecurity.

Purpose: These audits ensure that organizations fulfill mandatory external requirements established by regulatory authorities and industry guidelines.

Examples:

NIST Cybersecurity Framework: Organizations can undergo evaluations by criteria set by the National Institute of Standards and Technology (NIST) to maintain strong cybersecurity operations.

ISO/IEC 27001: This standard defines a methodical process for handling sensitive organizational information to maintain security and adhere to compliance requirements.

Benefits:

Help prevent legal consequences and financial penalties.

Build trust with clients and stakeholders through enhanced credibility.

2. Risk Assessment Audits

Definition: Risk assessment audits work to discover risks to organizational assets before analyzing them and determining their priorities.

Purpose: The purpose of risk assessment audits is to evaluate threats and establish proper mitigation plans.

Examples:

Qualitative Risk Assessments: These assessments depend on expert opinions to subjectively evaluate risk factors.

Quantitative Risk Assessments: Numerical values evaluate risk probability and consequences through established models like the FAIR framework.

Benefits:

Identifies critical vulnerabilities that could disrupt operations.

Guides resource allocation for risk mitigation.

3. Operational Audits

Definition: Operational audits serve to assess how well operational processes function within an organization.

Purpose: Operational practices must match security policies and procedures to maintain organizational security integrity.

Examples:

Examine the processes used in responding to and recovering from incidents.

The study examines how employee cybersecurity awareness training programs improve security knowledge.

Benefits:

Enhances the overall efficiency of security operations.

Integrates security practices into everyday operational activities.

4. Technical Audits

Definition: Technical audits examine organizations' cybersecurity defenses by reviewing their hardware systems, software applications and network setups.

Purpose: The process aims to detect weaknesses in technical systems which attackers could potentially exploit.

Examples:

Vulnerability Scanning: Nessus and Qualys tools help discover known vulnerabilities in both systems and applications.

Penetration Testing: Testing security defenses through simulated cyberattacks reveals existing vulnerabilities.

Benefits:

The analysis reveals specific technical vulnerabilities within system infrastructure.

Organizations can determine which security issues to address first by assessing the level of risk associated with each vulnerability.

5. Third-Party Audits

Definition: Independent third-party audits evaluate the cybersecurity protocols implemented by vendors or partners who supply products or services to a business entity.

Purpose: Third-party audits verify that external partners implement sufficient security measures to protect joint data systems which decreases supply chain vulnerability risks.

Examples:

Vendor Risk Assessments: Assess vendor security practices through evaluation of their incident response strategy as well as their data protection measures together with regulatory compliance checks.

Certification Reviews: Assess whether third-party vendors maintain pertinent security certifications like ISO 27001 or SOC 2 because these certifications demonstrate adherence to cybersecurity best practices.

Benefits:

Enhances trust and confidence in third-party relationships.

Minimizes threats from supply chain attacks which occur when one company's weaknesses impact other connected businesses.

Cybersecurity Audit Methodologies

Selecting an appropriate methodology is essential for ensuring effective cybersecurity audit results. Organizations can select from multiple cybersecurity audit methodologies which they often customize to address their unique requirements. The following section outlines standard methodologies that organizations utilize during cybersecurity audits.

1. Control-Based Audits

Definition: This methodology evaluates individual controls set up to reduce risks.

Approach:

Implement a structured control framework using examples such as CIS Controls or NIST SP 800-53.

Test each control and review related documentation to determine how effective each one is.

Benefits:

Offers a systematic method to discover security deficiencies.

Facilitates compliance with established standards.

2. Risk-Based Audits

Definition: In risk-based audits organizations assess potential operational risks through identification and evaluation.

Approach:

Rank risks through an evaluation of both their possible effects and their probability of occurrence.

Allocate audit resources to the areas that present the greatest risk to the organization.

Benefits:

The audit process adapts to fit the organization's distinct risk environment.

Allocates resources effectively to reduce the most significant risks faced by the organization.

3. Integrated Audits

Definition: Integrated audits merge compliance, operational and technical audit types into one comprehensive assessment of the organization’s cybersecurity posture.

Approach:

Review regulatory adherence in conjunction with operational performance evaluation and technical weakness assessment.

Encourage cross-department collaboration for a comprehensive view.

Benefits:

Provides a well-rounded analysis of cybersecurity effectiveness.

This approach encourages different organizational teams to establish effective communication links and achieve their work objectives together.

4. Continuous Auditing

Definition: Continuous auditing includes uninterrupted monitoring and review of organizational security systems.

Approach:

Employ automated tools to maintain regular evaluations of security controls and compliance standards.

Set up immediate notification systems to detect any breaches in security protocols.

Benefits:

Allows organizations to detect and address new threats as they arise.

Keeps abreast of the current security conditions within the organization.

Preparing for an OT Cybersecurity Audit

Organizations need to complete multiple preparatory actions before they begin an OT cybersecurity audit to guarantee its success. The audit gains efficiency from proper preparation which also results in more valuable findings.

1. Define the Audit Scope

Importance: Defining the audit scope precisely enables auditors to concentrate on essential systems and processes which results in a more manageable and effective audit process.

Steps:

Determine which operational technology systems will be part of the audit including examples such as SCADA systems and PLCs as well as sensors.

Choose between a comprehensive audit or a targeted evaluation of selected systems.

Solicit feedback from stakeholders to identify important areas of concern.

2. Gather Documentation

Importance: Extensive documentation is essential for supplying context to the audit and enabling successful assessment processes.

Steps:

Create a complete list of OT assets which should cover hardware elements as well as software applications and network infrastructure components.

Assemble all existing security policies along with incident response plans and previous audit reports.

The collection of network diagrams and system architecture documentation helps to reveal the connections between OT systems.

3. Engage Stakeholders

Importance: Audits achieve organizational alignment and effectively target important concerns when they include relevant stakeholders.

Steps:

Determine primary stakeholders by including members from IT staff through management and compliance officers and OT personnel.

Organize meetings to establish audit objectives and collect vulnerability information.

Develop a collaborative atmosphere that encourages stakeholders to openly exchange information.

4. Select Audit Tools and Frameworks

Importance: The selection of appropriate audit tools and frameworks enables auditors to perform their tasks more efficiently while improving the precision of their results.

Steps:

Identify vulnerability scanning applications such as Nessus and Qualys along with compliance assessment tools that support the audit's objectives.

Select applicable frameworks (such as NIST and ISO 27001) to define the evaluation standards.

Confirm that the chosen tools work properly within the OT environment.

5. Develop an Audit Plan

Importance: The audit plan must detail the methodology to use during the audit along with the timeline and necessary resources to enable all stakeholders to comprehend their assigned roles and responsibilities.

Steps:

Define Objectives: The audit objectives should be clearly defined to show how it will identify vulnerabilities and ensure compliance while improving the security posture.

Establish a Timeline: Develop a practical timeline which incorporates important milestones including the audit start and end dates combined with documentation review deadlines and planned dates for stakeholder meetings.

Allocate Resources: Designate team members to handle data collection, analysis and reporting tasks. The audit team needs to possess the appropriate skills and tools to execute their tasks effectively.

Communication Plan: Establish a systematic update schedule to keep stakeholders informed during the audit process while maintaining transparency and alignment.

Conducting the Audit

The audit process starts once all the preparation steps have been completed. The primary activities during this stage include data acquisition and examination of controls followed by detection of vulnerabilities within the OT environment.

1. Data Collection

Importance: The audit relies on thorough and precise data collection to function effectively.

Steps:

Interviews: Interview system administrators and operators who hold key positions to understand how operations and security measure's function.

Documentation Review: Evaluate current security policies together with incident response plans and past audit reports to gain insight into the present security situation.

Technical Assessments: Use vulnerability scanning tools to perform configuration evaluations of OT systems.

2. Assessing Controls

Importance: Assessing security controls enables the discovery of vulnerabilities and improvement opportunities.

Steps:

Control Testing: Determine how well technical controls including firewalls, intrusion detection systems and access controls perform. Make sure firewalls are set up properly to prevent unauthorized access.

Policy Evaluation: Evaluate how well the organization follows security policies through training programs and incident response protocols. Check whether employees possess the necessary training to detect cybersecurity incidents and execute appropriate responses.

Physical Security Assessment: Evaluate physical security systems like facility access controls for OT systems to confirm that they prevent unauthorized entry.

3. Vulnerability Identification

Importance: The identification of vulnerabilities plays a vital role in crafting successful remediation strategies.

Steps:

Vulnerability Scanning: Deploy automated tools to detect known vulnerabilities within OT systems. The security tool Nessus assists organizations by detecting obsolete software versions along with improperly configured systems.

Penetration Testing: Perform penetration tests under controlled conditions to mimic attacks targeting the OT environment. This process demonstrates the effectiveness of current defenses against simulated real-world attacks.

Reviewing Previous Incidents: Examine previous security incidents to discover patterns of vulnerabilities and recurring problems that require attention.

4. Analyzing Findings

Importance: Detailed examination of findings enables organizations to establish vulnerability priorities and develop effective remediation approaches.

Steps:

Categorization: Assigned severity levels to identified vulnerabilities according to their effect on operations. Employ the Common Vulnerability Scoring System (CVSS) or another standardized framework to assign vulnerability scores.

Root Cause Analysis: When facing critical vulnerabilities or incidents perform root cause analysis to identify the basic issues that create security weaknesses.

Stakeholder Involvement: Include relevant stakeholders in discussions about findings to collect their insights on potential impacts and remediation approaches.

Reporting

The next step after finishing the audit involves assembling all findings into a detailed report. The report serves as a crucial tool for delivering audit results to stakeholders while directing future security improvement plans.

1. Structuring the Audit Report

Importance: A report that follows a clear structure allows readers to understand important findings with greater ease.

Steps:

Executive Summary: Kick off the audit report with an executive summary that presents the primary objectives alongside key findings and overarching recommendations. The section needs to present information in a brief and understandable format suitable for management review.

Detailed Findings: Organize detailed findings according to specific categories including compliance checks and technical vulnerabilities assessment. All findings require documentation that explains both the specific issue and its potential consequences as well as the evidence obtained during the audit process.

Recommendations: Develop actionable steps to resolve detected security weaknesses and improve control measures. Organize recommendations starting with the highest risk levels alongside their potential operational impacts.

Appendices: Attach all relevant supporting documentation which includes the data collection tools used along with interview notes and vulnerability scan results.

2. Communicating Findings

Importance: When audit findings are communicated effectively, they generate comprehension and stimulate necessary actions.

Steps:

Stakeholder Presentation: Organize a meeting to go over audit results and suggestions with the main stakeholders. Key points become clearer to stakeholders when you present them using visual aids like charts and graphs.

Encourage Discussion: Create space for open discussion during the presentation to solicit stakeholder questions and feedback. This process leads to improved recommendations and secures stakeholder support.

Follow-Up Actions: Based on presentation discussions define follow-up actions while confirming stakeholder responsibilities for addressing audit findings.

3. Tracking Remediation Efforts

Importance: The implementation of recommendations requires ongoing monitoring to ensure that vulnerabilities discovered receive proper attention and resolution.

Steps:

Action Plans: Create comprehensive action plans for every recommendation by outlining required tasks along with assigned personnel and specified completion dates. When outdated software is identified through a vulnerability scan the action plan needs to specify update procedures, assign responsible staff members and establish completion deadlines.

Regular Check-Ins: Establish routine meetings with stakeholders to review remediation progress. Regular check-ins help sustain progress while allowing teams to troubleshoot emerging difficulties.

Documenting Changes: Maintain thorough documentation of every adjustment carried out because of audit findings which include policy updates and technical control enhancements. The documentation serves as an important resource for subsequent audits and assessments.

Continuous Improvement

Cybersecurity demands ongoing attention and development because it cannot be accomplished through a single action. Organizations should build a culture of security and update their cybersecurity practices regularly after completing the audit process.

1. Establishing a Cybersecurity Framework

Importance: Organizations can manage risks and enhance their security posture progressively through structured cybersecurity framework implementation.

Framework Examples:

NIST Cybersecurity Framework: The framework outlines procedures for recognizing cybersecurity threats as well as steps for protection and detection of incidents together with response and recovery processes.

ISO/IEC 27001: ISO/IEC 27001 provides an extensive strategy for information security management through risk assessment and control implementation followed by continuous improvement.

Steps:

Adopt a Framework: Select a cybersecurity framework which meets both organizational objectives and regulatory obligations.

Tailor the Framework: Modify the framework to ensure it matches the organization's particular requirements and operational environment by addressing distinct operational problems and risk assessments.

Training and Awareness: Train every employee in the selected framework so that they comprehend their responsibilities toward cybersecurity maintenance.

2. Regular Reviews and Updates

Importance: Ongoing assessment of cybersecurity protocols enables organizations to maintain resilience against new security threats.

Steps:

Scheduled Audits: Organizations must perform cybersecurity audits every year to evaluate security controls and discover new vulnerabilities.

Policy Reviews: Frequently revise security policies to align them with technological advancements, regulatory updates, and organizational practice changes.

Incident Review: Following any security incident organizations should perform a post-mortem analysis to determine failure points and extract lessons to improve security measures.

3. Engaging with the Cybersecurity Community

Importance: Working together with the cybersecurity community creates opportunities to gain useful insights and access shared resources.

Steps:

Participate in Industry Groups: Participate in industry-focused organizations and online forums to exchange knowledge about best practices and threat intelligence.

Attend Conferences and Workshops: Participate in cybersecurity conferences and workshops to keep abreast of emerging trends and technologies as well as new threats.

Collaborate on Research: Building partnerships with academic and research institutions can help progress OT cybersecurity knowledge.

Conclusion

Organizations operating in OT environments must understand and implement effective cybersecurity audits to protect their systems. In this chapter we examined cybersecurity audits by defining them and demonstrating their significance before outlining their different types and methodologies and finally detailing the preparation and reporting process.

Organizations boost their security measures and guarantee compliance when they evaluate OT system security posture systematically to discover vulnerabilities. The implementation of an ongoing improvement framework encourages the development of a proactive cybersecurity culture capable of responding to changing threats.

This handbook's subsequent sections will examine detailed strategies and best practices for OT cybersecurity audits with a focus on regulatory frameworks, risk assessments and incident response planning. These insights deliver essential tools to organizations for securing their OT environments while safeguarding critical infrastructure against cyber-attacks.

Chapter 2 of "The OT Cybersecurity Audit Handbook: Strategies for Success" reaches its conclusion here. The following chapters will address relevant regulatory frameworks for OT cybersecurity alongside risk management methodologies and practical security auditing tools that help organizations achieve better security in their operational environments.

Chapter 3: Regulatory Frameworks and Standards

Introduction

Regulatory frameworks and standards serve as essential components in Operational Technology (OT) cybersecurity by providing essential guidelines and best practices to protect critical infrastructure. These frameworks enable organizations to meet legal and regulatory standards while simultaneously strengthening their security measures. This chapter examines the crucial regulatory frameworks and standards for OT cybersecurity and discusses their importance while providing guidance on effective organizational implementation.

Importance of Regulatory Frameworks and Standards

1. Compliance and Legal Obligations

Critical sector organizations like those in energy, water, transportation and healthcare must adhere to stringent regulations designed to safeguard vital infrastructure against cyber threats. Organizations that fail to comply with regulations risk facing harsh penalties alongside potential legal issues and damage to their public image.

2. Establishing a Baseline

Through regulatory frameworks organizations gain access to predefined security requirements and best practice standards which support them in defining their cybersecurity baseline. The baseline serves as a critical tool for evaluating existing practices while pinpointing deficiencies to facilitate essential updates.

3. Enhancing Risk Management

Organizations can improve their risk management processes by following established standards. Through regulatory frameworks organizations can discover possible weaknesses and dangers which allow them to direct their cybersecurity initiatives appropriately.

4. Building Trust with Stakeholders

An organization's credibility grows along with trust from customers and partners when it meets recognized standards and maintains compliance with regulatory bodies. Organizations that show dedication to cybersecurity stand out from their competitors in the marketplace.

Key Regulatory Frameworks and Standards

Our discussion will cover the leading regulatory frameworks and standards that apply to OT cybersecurity.

1. NIST Cybersecurity Framework (NIST CSF)

Overview: The NIST Cybersecurity Framework establishes a policy structure that guides U.S. private sector organizations in evaluating and enhancing their capabilities to thwart, identify, and address cyber-attacks.

Key Components:

Framework Core: The framework's foundation includes five essential functions: Identify, Protect, Detect, Respond, and Recover. Every function offers an overarching perspective of the stages involved in cybersecurity program operation.

Implementation Tiers: The implementation tiers enable organizations to assess their cybersecurity practices' maturity and readiness levels.

Profiles: Organizations could develop profiles that match their business objectives, risk preferences, and available resources.

Benefits:

The NIST CSF offers adaptable guidelines which organizations from different sizes and sectors including OT environments can customize.

The framework provides a shared terminology for organizations to discuss cybersecurity risks and practices.

Example Implementation: By implementing the NIST CSF an energy company can evaluate its cybersecurity standing while pinpointing essential assets and formulating a strategic plan to boost security throughout its OT systems.

2. ISO/IEC 27001

Overview: ISO/IEC 27001 sets international standards detailing how to create an information security management system (ISMS) and maintain its continuous improvement.

Key Components:

Risk Assessment: Organizations need to detect and evaluate security risks that affect their information assets.

Management Commitment: Senior executives need to show strong leadership and dedication to the information security management system.

Continuous Improvement: The standard requires organizations to constantly evaluate and enhance their security measures.

Benefits:

Organizations that obtain ISO/IEC 27001 certification improve their marketability while showing dedication to maintaining information security.

The framework presents an all-encompassing method to handle sensitive information while maintaining adherence to multiple regulatory standards.

Example Implementation: Manufacturing companies achieve ISO/IEC 27001 implementation through comprehensive OT system risk assessments, ISMS establishment and consistent security policy updates that reflect current threats.

3. IEC 62443

Overview: The IEC 62443 series represent international standards that target cybersecurity protection for industrial automation and control systems (IACS). This system offers a complete framework solution for the protection of OT environments.

Key Components:

General Requirements: This standard defines security levels for industrial control systems and specifies necessary protective measures.

System Requirements: The standard specifies security protocols for multiple system elements including both hardware components and software applications.

Product Requirements: This standard sets mandatory security requirements for IACS products which ensure security is integrated into their design.

Benefits:

IEC 62443 offers a systematic method to protect industrial control systems which makes it vital for organizations working in manufacturing, energy production and water treatment sectors.

The framework allows organizations to adjust their cybersecurity strategies to meet established industry standards and best practices.

Example: To implement IEC 62443 a water treatment facility must evaluate control systems to find vulnerabilities before installing essential security controls to defend against cyber threats.

4. NERC CIP Standards

Overview: The North American Electric Reliability Corporation's Critical Infrastructure Protection (CIP) standards protect the bulk electric system's cybersecurity throughout North America. Organizations that own or operate electric power grid elements must follow these standards.

Key Components:

CIP-002: The standard requires organizations to classify critical assets and systems according to their impact on the electric grid's reliability.

CIP-003: Security management controls mandate organizations to create and execute a cybersecurity plan according to this standard.

CIP-004: This standard implements personnel training and security awareness programs to equip staff with the necessary skills to identify and react to cyber threats.

CIP-006: Physical security strategies protect essential assets by preventing unauthorized entry.

Benefits:

NERC CIP standards enable utilities to adopt comprehensive security measures against cyber threats through proactive operational security strategies.

Upholding these standards is fundamental to preserve system dependability and prevent regulatory consequences.

Example Implementation: Electric utility companies can meet NERC CIP requirements through consistent evaluations of important assets alongside strong access control implementation and regular cybersecurity employee training.

5. GDPR (General Data Protection Regulation)

Overview: GDPR serves as a complete data protection regulation within the European Union to control how personal data is processed. Its focus is data privacy, yet it creates significant impacts on cybersecurity practices.

Key Components:

Data Protection by Design and by Default: Organizations need to establish mechanisms that incorporate data protection into their data processing activities.

Data Breach Notification: If a data breach threatens individual rights and freedoms organizations must report it to authorities within 72 hours.

Accountability and Governance: Organizations need to show regulatory compliance by maintaining appropriate documentation which may lead to inspections from oversight agencies.

Benefits:

Adhering to GDPR requirements enables personal data protection while simultaneously fortifying organizational security through improved data management and cybersecurity best practices.

The regulation improves visibility and develops customer and stakeholder confidence.

Example Implementation: By conducting data protection impact assessments (DPIAs) technology firms that handle personal data of EU citizens can implement GDPR through appropriate technical and organizational measures that protect personal data.

6. HIPAA (Health Insurance Portability and Accountability Act)

Overview: The Health Insurance Portability and Accountability Act establishes United States standards to protect sensitive patient health data. Organizations operating within the healthcare sector find this information particularly relevant.

Key Components:

Administrative Safeguards: Organizations need to establish procedures and policies to oversee security measure selection, development, and maintenance.

Physical Safeguards: Electronic systems and data need security measures to prevent unauthorized access.

Technical Safeguards: Healthcare organizations need to enforce technological protections to safeguard electronic health information (ePHI) while managing access rights.

Benefits:

By following HIPAA guidelines healthcare organizations can secure patient data and decrease data breach risks while preserving patient trust.

The framework focuses on managing cybersecurity risks within healthcare institutions.

Example Implementation: Healthcare providers achieve HIPAA compliance through routine risk assessments and electronic health records access controls alongside continuous staff training in data privacy and security matters.

Implementing Regulatory Frameworks and Standards

A structured approach is necessary to implement regulatory frameworks and standards successfully in OT environments. This section outlines the required actions organizations should follow to successfully incorporate these frameworks into their cybersecurity practices.

1. Conduct a Gap Analysis

Importance: Organizations can evaluate their existing cybersecurity approaches in relation to regulatory framework requirements through gap analysis.

Steps:

Identify Relevant Frameworks: Organizations should identify which regulatory frameworks and standards apply to their operations by analyzing their specific industry and geographical location.

Assess Current Practices: Examine existing organizational policies alongside procedures and controls to detect compliance deficiencies.

Document Findings: Prepare a gap analysis report which includes prioritized improvement areas based on both risk and impact assessments.

2. Develop an Implementation Plan

Importance: The implementation plan acts as a strategic guide to close compliance gaps while improving cybersecurity defense measures.

Steps:

Set Objectives: Establish specific targets for compliance and security enhancements by interpreting the gap analysis findings.

Allocate Resources: Determine essential resources such as personnel, budget allocations and technological tools required for implementation.

Establish Timelines: Develop a detailed timeline to guide the implementation of suggested improvements and changes.

3. Engage Stakeholders

Importance: Stakeholder engagement generates organizational support for implementation while informing all parties involved about their specific roles.

Steps:

Identify Key Stakeholders: Your implementation team should consist of representatives from IT, OT, compliance, management functions along with members from any pertinent departments. The establishment of such a team leads to a cross-functional group that approaches cybersecurity through various angles.

Communicate Objectives: Make sure that stakeholders understand why the organization is introducing regulatory frameworks and standards. Describe how these initiatives will improve both the organization's security posture and its risk management approach.

Foster Collaboration: Stakeholders should work together to exchange insights and address concerns while generating solutions through brainstorming. Regular meetings help sustain participant involvement while keeping everyone focused on shared objectives.

4. Train Employees

Importance: Effective employee training ensures staff understand their responsibilities for compliance and security maintenance.

Steps:

Develop Training Programs: Develop training content that incorporates both regulatory standards and organizational policies and procedures.

Conduct Regular Training Sessions: All employees must have scheduled training sessions with a specific focus on staff members who work within OT and cybersecurity functions. Design training modules that match the specific responsibilities of each organizational position.

Assess Knowledge Retention: Evaluate employee comprehension of training content through assessments or quizzes. The assessments help strengthen crucial concepts while revealing areas that need further attention.

5. Implement Technical Controls

Importance: Technical controls play a crucial role in maintaining compliance and defending OT systems against cyber threats.

Steps:

Access Controls: Restrict access to essential systems and data through role-based access control (RBAC) according to the job duties of personnel. Access to control systems and sensitive data must be limited to authorized personnel only.

Encryption: Implement encryption to secure sensitive information during transmission and when it is stored. Compliance with regulatory standards demands heightened protection for personal information regulated by GDPR and HIPAA.

Monitoring and Logging: Implement monitoring and logging systems to identify security threats and take immediate action against them. Automated systems enable organizations to monitor system access and identify suspicious behavior.

6. Establish Policies and Procedures

Importance: Well-defined policies and procedures create a framework that helps organizations meet regulatory requirements while maintaining secure operations.

Steps:

Develop Comprehensive Security Policies: Formulate organizational cybersecurity policies which define procedures for data protection together with incident response and access control measures.

Document Procedures: Establish procedures that provide guidance on executing policies in real-world applications. The documentation process encompasses comprehensive guides for incident response and regular security evaluation procedures.

Review and Update Regularly: Put into place an evaluation system for policies and procedures which keeps them up-to-date and applicable in response to changes in regulations and emerging threats.

7. Conduct Regular Audits and Assessments

Importance: Evaluating implemented controls and verifying adherence to regulatory standards demands ongoing audits and assessments.

Steps:

Schedule Audits: Establish a routine schedule for internal audits to evaluate adherence to established policies and procedures. Regular evaluations will reveal opportunities for enhancement while maintaining consistent regulatory compliance.

Engage Third-Party Assessors: Hire external experts to evaluate your compliance and security measures from an independent standpoint. External auditors or consultants offer important insights while pinpointing compliance gaps that internal teams might miss.

Document Findings and Remediation Efforts: Document all audit findings along with remediation actions taken and any improvements made as a result. Organizations must maintain documentation because it serves as proof of compliance during regulatory inspections.

Challenges in Implementing Regulatory Frameworks

As regulatory frameworks and standards offer substantial benefits organizations need to implement them must also navigate multiple challenges throughout the implementation process. Organizations can develop effective strategies to overcome implementation challenges by understanding them.

1. Resource Limitations

Challenge: Smaller organizations commonly encounter constraints in budget, personnel, and time resources.

Strategies:

Prioritize Initiatives: Organizations should direct their compliance and security efforts to the most crucial areas identified through risk assessments. Organizations can manage their resources efficiently while avoiding resource exhaustion by following this approach.

Leverage Existing Resources: Organizations can implement compliance measures by making use of their present personnel and available technologies. The current IT team members can receive education to fulfill the cybersecurity requirements of OT systems.

2. Complexity of Regulations

Challenge: The complexity and extensive scope of multiple regulations present overwhelming challenges for organizations.

Strategies:

Engage Legal and Compliance Experts: Consult legal and compliance professionals who hold expertise in necessary regulations to receive their guidance. They provide detailed explanations of requirements while offering practical strategies for implementation.

Develop a Compliance Roadmap: Develop a roadmap that explains how to achieve compliance with various regulations through manageable tasks.

3. Resistance to Change

Challenge: Workers tend to oppose alterations to their routine procedures when they view newly implemented policies as burdensome.

Strategies:

Communicate the Benefits: Demonstrate how compliance and improved security systems benefit both the company and its workforce. These security measures defend both organizational structures and individual job functions against cyber threats.

Involve Employees in the Process: Involve employees in creating new organizational protocols and procedures. When organizations ask for employee feedback, they create a sense of ownership over new changes which help minimize opposition.

Provide Support and Resources: Adequate training and support must be provided to enable employees to adjust to new work practices. Easing the transition for employees while building their confidence depends on making resources available to them.

4. Keeping Up with Evolving Regulations

Challenge: Because regulatory landscapes are always changing organizations find it hard to remain compliant.

Strategies:

Establish a Compliance Team: Organizations should create a specialized compliance team whose responsibility includes monitoring regulatory changes and evaluating their effects on the organization. The dedicated team must track updates to relevant regulations and frameworks to remain informed.

Regular Training and Updates: Create continuous training programs that keep employees up to date with changes in regulations and compliance requirements. This can include workshops, webinars, or newsletters.

5. Integration with Existing Systems

Challenge: The process of merging new compliance requirements into current systems proves difficult for organizations that use outdated legacy systems.

Strategies:

Conduct a System Inventory: Start by performing an extensive review of current systems to identify necessary changes. This can help identify potential integration challenges.

Adopt a Phased Approach: Introduce compliance measures through a phased implementation instead of applying them all simultaneously. Testing and refining processes through this approach allows easier integration of new measures with existing systems.

Conclusion

The foundation of a strong OT cybersecurity strategy includes regulatory frameworks and standards. Organizations can strengthen their security measures and meet legal requirements while earning stakeholder trust by thoroughly understanding and applying these frameworks.

This chapter examined essential regulatory frameworks consisting of the NIST Cybersecurity Framework, ISO/IEC 27001, IEC 62443, NERC CIP standards, GDPR, and HIPAA. These frameworks offer essential guidelines and best practices to secure critical infrastructure and handle cybersecurity risks.

Our discussion included actionable methods for applying these frameworks which involved gap analyses execution and both stakeholder engagement along with employee training programs. Achieving long-term success requires organizations to recognize and address implementation challenges.

The subsequent chapters will present thorough investigations into risk assessment methodologies together with management approaches and explain tools and techniques necessary for successful OT cybersecurity audits. Through providing organizations with essential knowledge and resources to manage OT cybersecurity challenges we create a more secure and robust operational framework.

Chapter 3 of "The OT Cybersecurity Audit Handbook: Strategies for Success" has reached its conclusion. The next sections will delve into risk management approaches alongside cybersecurity audit best practices and actionable solutions for securing operational technology systems. The insights presented will enable organizations to build strong defenses that protect critical infrastructure from modern cyber threats.

Chapter 4: Preparing for an OT Cybersecurity Audit

Introduction

An effective Operational Technology (OT) cybersecurity audit starts with proper preparation which establishes the basis for assessing an organization's security status. Operational Technology systems function with distinct constraints and requirements different from traditional IT environments which require specialized preparation approaches. The chapter presents the critical steps required for OT cybersecurity audit preparation which involves scope definition, documentation collection, stakeholder engagement, audit tool selection, and audit plan creation.

Defining the Audit Scope

Importance of Scope Definition

Establishing the audit scope stands out as a fundamental preparation step that must be prioritized. Establishing an audit scope enables focused examination of essential systems and processes which leads to efficient resource utilization and meaningful audit results.

Steps to Define the Scope

Identify Systems and Assets:

Inventory OT Systems: Construct a complete list of all OT systems that need to be evaluated during the audit. The audit scope normally consists of Supervisory Control and Data Acquisition (SCADA) systems together with Programmable Logic Controllers (PLCs), Human-Machine Interfaces (HMIs), sensors and other networked devices.

Assess Criticality: Assess each system's importance to operational processes through collaboration with stakeholders. Organizations should give priority to systems essential for safety operations as well as those required to ensure compliance and maintain business continuity.

Determine the Audit Objectives:

Compliance vs. Risk Assessment: Select whether the audit will concentrate on regulatory compliance (such as NERC CIP, IEC 62443) or focus on discovering and managing risks. The chosen focus of the audit determines which methodology and tools will be implemented.

Stakeholder Input: Collect input from stakeholders regarding their specific audit concerns and objectives. A production manager will likely prioritize the security of systems which affect operational efficiency.

Set Boundaries:

Inclusions and Exclusions: The audit report should specify which elements will be examined and which will remain outside its scope. When conducting a SCADA system audit it is important to define whether peripheral systems like data historians and reporting tools will be included in the assessment.

Physical Considerations: Consider geographical and physical boundaries. When conducting audits with multiple facilities indicate specifically which locations will be included in the audit scope.

Example of Audit Scope

A sample of a precise audit scope description could appear as follows:

The cybersecurity audit will assess the SCADA system at the water treatment facility as well as all integrated PLCs, HMIs, and remote monitoring tools. This audit will examine adherence to NERC CIP standards and determine system vulnerabilities that threaten operational safety. The scope will not include peripheral systems like data storage and reporting tools.

Gathering Documentation

Importance of Documentation

It is essential to maintain comprehensive documentation to ensure context and clarity throughout the audit process.

Through complete documentation auditors acquire full knowledge of the systems along with their policies and procedures which allows them to perform a comprehensive evaluation.

Types of Documentation to Gather

Asset Inventory:

Hardware and Software Inventory: Assemble a comprehensive inventory for all hardware and software elements utilized in the OT systems. The documentation must contain information about version numbers as well as configurations and patch levels.

Network Diagrams:

Visual Representation: Develop comprehensive network diagrams that show the connection pathways between OT systems. The diagrams must display communication pathways and firewall placements along with external IT system connections.

Security Policies and Procedures:

Existing Policies: Compile every pertinent security policy which encompasses access control policies together with incident response plans and data protection protocols. All documents must contain current information and show today's standard operational procedures.

Previous Audit Reports:

Historical Context: Collect audit reports from previous evaluations of OT systems. These reports serve as important resources to understand previous security weaknesses and evaluate how past remediation actions are performed.

Regulatory Compliance Documentation:

Evidence of Compliance: Assemble records to verify adherence to applicable regulatory and standard requirements. The evidence of compliance should feature certification letters alongside compliance checklists and risk assessments.

Organizing Documentation

Centralizing documentation organization helps streamline the audit process. The audit team needs immediate access to all relevant documents which should be stored in a shared folder or document management system.

Engaging Stakeholders

Importance of Stakeholder Engagement

The audit process requires stakeholder engagement to ensure both organizational goal alignment and full party participation. Input from stakeholders helps to identify important challenges and concerns specific to OT cybersecurity.

Steps to Engage Stakeholders

Identify Key Stakeholders:

Cross-Functional Team: Select members from IT, OT, compliance, and management departments who need to participate in the audit. The audit process will benefit from the different viewpoints of all participants.

2. Schedule Initial Meetings

Kick-off Meeting: Convene a kick-off meeting with essential stakeholders to outline the audit's objectives together with its scope and timeline. The initial meeting must establish a collaborative atmosphere while defining expectations.

Regular Check-Ins: Set up consistent meeting dates to maintain regular check-ins during the entire audit period. This approach maintains constant communication and gives stakeholders the opportunity to share input and solve any emerging issues.

3. Foster a Culture of Openness

Encourage Feedback: Develop a setting where stakeholders can freely express their insights and share any concerns they might have. Inform stakeholders their input plays a crucial role in identifying potential security weaknesses and enhancing security measures.

Address Concerns: Actively engage with stakeholder concerns throughout the audit process. It may involve explaining the purpose of audit findings or ensuring stakeholders that sensitive data will be managed properly.

4. Assign Roles and Responsibilities

Define Roles: Define in detail the roles and responsibilities that each stakeholder will have throughout the audit process. The technical documentation responsibility falls on IT personnel as OT staff focus on sharing operational practices knowledge.

Point of Contact: Select one person to be the main point of contact for the audit team. The designated individual will facilitate communication between auditors and stakeholders to guarantee effective coordination.

Example of Stakeholder Engagement

Effective stakeholder engagement is illustrated through these specific actions.

The audit team conducted an initial meeting with IT, OT, compliance, and management team representatives. The team presented the audit objectives during the meeting which covered the assessment of IEC 62443 standards compliance and identification of SCADA system vulnerabilities. The audit team established biweekly meetings to review progress and obtain stakeholder feedback. The team stressed the need for open communication and motivated stakeholders to express their insights and concerns during the process.

Selecting Audit Tools

Importance of Tools Selection

The audit process demands careful selection of appropriate tools to ensure both comprehensive coverage and efficient performance. Proper tools enable efficient data collection automation while supporting vulnerability assessments and improving the reporting procedure.

Types of Tools to Consider

Vulnerability Scanners:

Purpose: These tools autonomously examine OT systems to detect recognized vulnerabilities and configuration errors. These tools function as indicators of vulnerabilities which cyber adversaries can target.

Examples: The widely used vulnerability scanners Nessus, Qualys, and Rapid7 perform essential scanning tasks.

Configuration Management Tools:

Purpose: Configuration management tools evaluate device and system setups to see how well they follow established security standards. These tools check the OT systems to make sure they adhere to security standards and proper configurations.

Examples: CIS-CAT and Tripwire serve as helpful tools for evaluating system configurations.

Network Monitoring Tools:

Purpose: The tools analyze network traffic to detect anomalies or potential security incidents. The tools deliver information about communication patterns that exist within the OT environment.

Examples: SolarWinds and Darktrace help with network monitoring and detecting threats.

Risk Assessment Tools:

Purpose: Risk assessment tools help organizations find and analyze potential system and data vulnerabilities.

Examples: The FAIR (Factor Analysis of Information Risk) and OCTAVE (Operationally Critical Threat, Asset, and Vulnerability Evaluation) frameworks serve as guides for conducting risk assessments.

Considerations for Tool Selection

Compatibility: Confirm selected tools work with the existing OT systems and technologies used by the organization. The evaluation process should determine if the chosen tools can analyze proprietary systems or legacy technologies effectively.

Ease of Use: Consider the usability of the tools. Audit teams can work more efficiently and learn essential skills faster when tools have user-friendly interfaces and detailed documentation.

Cost: Evaluate tool pricing based on their functionality and feature set. The functionality of tools must align with financial limitations.

Developing an Audit Plan

Importance of an Audit Plan

The audit plan functions as a guide for the audit process by detailing the methodology to follow as well as the timeline and resources needed. A properly organized audit plan drives systematic and efficient audit execution which reduces interference with regular business activities.

Components of an Audit Plan

Objectives and Scope:

Clearly Defined Goals: The preliminary objectives and audit scope should be reviewed and reiterated as defined during the initial preparation phase. The foundation for the entire audit process begins here.

Methodology:

Audit Approach: Describe the audit's approach by specifying which assessment types will be conducted during the process including vulnerability scanning, interviews, and documentation review.

Risk-Based Focus: If relevant explain how a risk-based approach will be used to identify high-priority assessment areas through analysis of both criticality and risk exposure.

Timeline:

Milestone Schedule: The timeline should contain important milestones including start and end dates as well as deadlines for data gathering and stakeholder meeting and findings presentation dates. The timeline maintains audit progress while enforcing accountability.

Resource Allocation:

Team Roles: Establish explicit roles and responsibilities for each member of the audit team. Determine which team members will handle tasks related to data collection alongside analysis, documentation, and reporting responsibilities.

Resource Needs: The audit requires additional resources including specific tools or systems and support from IT or other departments.

Communication Strategy:

Reporting Schedule: Describe the timing and process for delivering progress reports to stakeholders. Frequent progress reports ensure stakeholder engagement and audit transparency throughout the entire process.

Feedback Mechanisms: Explain the methods for gathering stakeholder feedback and integrating their input into the audit process. Data collection methods could consist of structured interviews along with surveys and informal dialogues.

Example of an Audit Plan

The structure of an audit plan could appear as follows:

The audit will assess the cybersecurity status of the SCADA system at the water treatment facility by examining adherence to NERC CIP standards and pinpointing system weaknesses. The audit process will integrate vulnerability scanning techniques with documentation reviews and stakeholder interviews. The audit process will start on [start date] and end by [end date]. The audit will reach important steps when data collection finishes by [date], findings are shared with stakeholders on [date], and the audit report is submitted by [date]. Members from the IT, OT, and compliance departments will constitute the audit team with [team member name] as the primary point of contact.

Conducting Pre-Audit Activities

Executing pre-audit activities before starting the audit establishes the groundwork for a seamless and productive audit process. The initial activities establish a solid foundation for both data collection and analysis to be performed effectively.

1. Initial System Assessment

Importance: A preliminary assessment of targeted systems for auditing enables the identification of pressing issues and areas that need specialized focus.

Steps:

Preliminary Vulnerability Scan: Carry out an initial scan of OT systems to detect visible vulnerabilities and configuration errors. The audit can concentrate its efforts on the most important areas through this process.

Review System Health: Evaluate system health by inspecting outdated software, hardware malfunctions and connectivity challenges which could affect audit results.

2. Prepare the Audit Team

Importance: The audit team must have thorough preparation and system knowledge to execute a successful audit.

Steps:

Training Sessions: Hold training sessions to train the audit team on the specific OT systems and tools and methodologies they will use during the audit.

Technical Familiarization: The audit team should visit the OT environment and connect with key personnel if this step becomes necessary. The activity delivers essential context and insights into operational procedures.

3. Establish Baseline Metrics

Importance: Setting baseline metrics prior to the audit serves as an essential reference point to assess security control efficiency.

Steps:

Identify Key Performance Indicators (KPIs): Identify metrics that will aid in evaluating the security posture of OT systems. Typical key performance indicators involve the count of discovered vulnerabilities, the duration needed to fix vulnerabilities, and adherence to established security policies.

Collect Initial Data: Collect initial data for these metrics to create a baseline that enables comparison after the audit.

Conclusion

An OT cybersecurity audit demands careful planning and coordination throughout its multifaceted preparation process. Organizations establish groundwork for successful audit execution by defining audit scope and collecting necessary documentation while involving relevant stakeholders and choosing the right tools and developing detailed audit plans.

This chapter outlined the necessary procedures for OT cybersecurity audit preparation while stressing the need for specific goals, proper communication channels, and complete documentation. Organizations that implement these preparatory actions will achieve better audit results while identifying system weaknesses and enhancing their security framework.

The upcoming chapters address both risk assessment methodologies and audit execution techniques along with best practices for applying audit results to improve OT cybersecurity defenses. Organizations can use these insights to create effective defenses for their critical infrastructure against evolving cyber threats.

Chapter 4 of "The OT Cybersecurity Audit Handbook: Strategies for Success" ends here. The upcoming chapters will further investigate various OT cybersecurity audit techniques alongside risk management best practices and operational security improvement tools. Organizations can effectively manage OT cybersecurity challenges by employing these strategies which enable them to construct strong defenses against possible threats.

Chapter 5: Risk Assessment and Management in OT Cybersecurity

Introduction

The growing complexity of cyber threats makes risk assessment and management essential elements of any successful cybersecurity approach, especially within Operational Technology (OT) settings. Operational Technology (OT) systems stand apart from traditional IT systems because they connect to essential physical processes which require top-level security measures. The chapter examines OT cybersecurity risk assessment principles together with assessment methodologies and explores strategies to manage identified risks.

Understanding Risk in OT Environments

What is Risk?

Cybersecurity risk represents potential harm or loss resulting from a threat exploiting system vulnerabilities. The formula below summarizes how threat interacts with vulnerability and impact to determine risk.

Risk = Threat x Vulnerability x Impact

Threat: Any activity or occurrence that poses a threat to the organization's resources and business functions. Potential threats to an organization comprise cyberattacks along with natural disasters and insider threats.

Vulnerability: Vulnerabilities refer to system weaknesses or control failures that attackers can take advantage of to compromise security. The existence of outdated software together with inadequate security policies and insufficient employee training creates vulnerabilities.

Impact: A successful exploit could lead to financial loss along with operational disruption and reputational damage as well as regulatory penalties.

Unique Challenges of OT Cybersecurity

The specific difficulties found in OT settings make risk assessment and management processes complex.

Legacy Systems: OT systems often rely on outdated technology which fails to support current security protocols thus exposing them to greater security risks.

Safety Concerns: OT cyber events can lead to immediate physical hazards which might put human lives at risk while simultaneously causing extensive damage to infrastructure.

Integration with IT: The merging of IT and OT systems broadens the attack surface which requires an expanded risk management strategy.

Regulatory Requirements: Critical sector organizations are required to follow multiple regulations that enforce specific cybersecurity practices which complicate their risk assessment processes.

The Risk Assessment Process

A complete risk assessment for operational technology contexts requires multiple essential stages. The risk assessment process demands each step to address vulnerabilities identification and impact evaluation while creating effective risk mitigation strategies.

Step 1: Asset Identification

Importance: Risk assessment begins with the identification and classification of every asset that exists in the OT environment. The risk management process depends entirely on understanding which assets need protection.

Actions:

Create an Asset Inventory: Generate a complete inventory of all OT assets that encompasses hardware (e.g., PLCs, sensors), software (e.g., SCADA systems), and network components (e.g., routers, switches).

Categorize Assets: Group assets according to their essential role in operational processes. High-priority assets consist of those which perform essential functions along with assets that carry significant safety implications.

Example: A manufacturing facility's critical assets comprise the SCADA system which manages production processes along with safety interlocks and equipment communication systems.

Step 2: Threat Identification

Importance: Through threat identification organizations gain knowledge about potential exploiters of their OT system vulnerabilities.

Actions:

Conduct Threat Modeling: Apply threat modeling techniques for discovering potential threats that affect OT environments.

Potential threats could arise from both outside sources such as cybercriminals and nation-state actors and inside sources like disgruntled employees.

Evaluate Historical Data: Perform an analysis of previous incidents from both organizational and industry sources to determine common threat vectors and scenarios that pose risks to OT systems.

Example: Through threat modeling exercises manufacturing facilities may discover susceptibility to ransomware attacks when employee training on phishing detection proves insufficient.

Step 3: Vulnerability Assessment

Importance: Through vulnerability assessments organizations pinpoint system weaknesses that identified threats could exploit.

Actions:

Conduct Vulnerability Scans: Deploy automated scanning tools to detect known vulnerabilities and configuration errors in OT systems. Security tools such as Nessus and Qualys assist in detecting security problems within both hardware and software components.

Perform Manual Assessments: Manual assessments should complement automated scans to detect vulnerabilities that automated tools often overlook, including weak physical security controls and insufficient employee training.

Example: A scan of vulnerabilities may show that certain PLCs operate with old firmware versions which makes them vulnerable to established exploits.

Step 4: Impact Analysis

Importance: Organizations need to understand the potential effects of identified risks to effectively prioritize mitigation actions.

Actions:

Assess Business Impact: Analyze how a successful security breach might impact business functions through financial loss, operational interruptions and reputational harm.

Consider Safety Implications: In OT system evaluations you need to examine how risks might affect human safety and lead to environmental damage.

Example: A cyberattack on the SCADA system analysis could show substantial operational downtime which would lead to production losses and safety risks for employees.

Step 4: Impact Analysis (continued)

Example: A cyber breach impacts the chemical dosing system within a water treatment facility. The impact analysis shows improper chemical dosing results in regulatory fines while endangering public health and safety which makes this risk extremely critical.

Step 5: Risk Evaluation

Importance: The evaluation process for identified risks requires organizations to assess their importance and establish a priority order for mitigation strategies. Through this step organizations learn to direct their resources towards mitigating the most severe vulnerabilities.

Actions:

Risk Rating: Evaluate each identified risk by assigning a rating that reflects both the probability of it happening and how severe its consequences are. The typical risk assessment scales consist of low, medium, high, and critical levels.

Risk Matrix: A risk matrix serves as a visual tool that demonstrates how the probability of an event relates to its potential effects enabling quick detection of major risks.

Example: An outdated firewall presents a risk that receives a high likelihood and high impact rating because it can enable unauthorized access to essential systems. A minor defect in an application that doesn't handle critical functions will typically receive both low likelihood and low impact ratings.

Step 6: Risk Treatment

Importance: The last step of risk assessment requires organizations to decide treatment strategies for the risks they have identified. The risk treatment step requires determining whether each risk should be mitigated, transferred, accepted or avoided.

Actions:

Develop Mitigation Strategies: Create targeted mitigation plans for risks that are considered high priority. The mitigation process may include the adoption of technical controls alongside the improvement of policies and procedures and the delivery of further training sessions.

Risk Transfer: Organizations sometimes transfer risk by purchasing insurance or by outsourcing specific functions through third-party service providers.

Accepting Risk: Organizations will accept low-priority risks when they choose to monitor these risks over time as long as these risks do not present a major operational threat.

Avoiding Risk: When risks become too severe organizations may decide to remove vulnerable processes or systems to avoid exposure.

Example: Organizations implement patches and updates as a mitigation strategy when a critical vulnerability emerges in their SCADA system. An organization may decide to track a minor software vulnerability without taking immediate action when they determine that the risk is acceptable.

Organizations develop mitigation techniques to address rising risks from cyber threats.

Risk Management Strategies in OT Cybersecurity

After organizations determine which risks to prioritize, they need to apply efficient risk management strategies to both lower their exposure and strengthen security defenses.

1. Implementing Technical Controls

Importance: Technical controls play a crucial role in protecting OT systems from cyber threats.

Actions:

Access Control Measures: Restrict access to critical systems through job-specific access controls. Only personnel with proper authorization should gain access to sensitive information and systems.

Network Segmentation: Protect OT systems by implementing network segmentation to physically isolate them from IT network infrastructure. Reducing the attack surface helps to limit the potential damage resulting from cyber incidents.

Regular Patching and Updates: Update and patch all hardware and software components regularly to protect against known security vulnerabilities.

Example: The manufacturing facility protects against unauthorized system access by requiring employees to use multi-factor authentication when they access the SCADA system.

2. Developing Policies and Procedures

Importance: Defined policies and procedures provide the essential structure for managing cybersecurity threats while maintaining regulatory compliance.

Actions:

Incident Response Plan: Establish an extensive incident response plan which details the steps necessary for identifying cyber incidents and outlines the response and recovery process. The plan must define roles and responsibilities together with communication protocols and recovery steps.

Security Awareness Training: Organize consistent cybersecurity training sessions to instruct employees about possible threats and protective measures that enhance security. The training program needs to cover phishing awareness and secure techniques for operating OT systems.

Change Management Procedures: Develop change management processes that mandate security evaluations for all OT system modifications prior to their implementation.

Example: Through regular employee training sessions on phishing recognition and suspicious activity reporting water utilities improve their organizational security awareness.

3. Conducting Regular Security Audits

Importance: Ongoing security evaluations play a crucial role in assessing control performance and discovering opportunities for system enhancement.

Actions:

Scheduled Audits: Perform routine audits on OT systems to verify adherence to security policies and discover potential system vulnerabilities. A full assessment requires the expertise of both internal and external auditing teams.

Continuous Monitoring: Use continuous monitoring solutions to identify anomalies and potential threats as they happen. Employing this proactive strategy enables organizations to detect and respond to incidents more quickly.

Example: An energy company should establish regular annual security audits of its OT systems while employing continuous monitoring solutions that notify the security team about unauthorized access attempts.

4. Engaging with the Cybersecurity Community

Importance: Organizations that work with industry colleagues and join cybersecurity initiatives improve their knowledge about current threats and effective security practices.

Actions:

Information Sharing: Enroll in sector-specific groups and discussion panels to exchange the best practices and threat-related information with your professional network. Through this partnership, organizations will gain valuable insights about shared vulnerabilities and how to mitigate them effectively.

Participate in Training and Workshops: Participate in OT cybersecurity training activities and conferences. These events enable participants to learn about current threats and technologies as well as new regulatory changes.

Collaborate with Government and Regulatory Bodies: Engage with government agencies and regulatory bodies to obtain the latest updates on compliance requirements and best practices. This process involves participating in public-private partnerships designed to enhance security measures within critical infrastructure sectors.

Example: By joining a local cybersecurity consortium transportation companies can share threat intelligence and best practices with other sector organizations to improve security awareness and preparedness.

5. Establishing a Culture of Security

Importance: Risk management efforts can only achieve long-term success when organizations maintain a robust security culture.

Actions:

Leadership Commitment: Leadership must show clear support for cybersecurity initiatives. Organizations should maintain ongoing discussions about security significance while directing funding toward education programs and technological solutions.

Employee Involvement: Mobilize employees to support cybersecurity initiatives by forming security champions or committees that spread the best security practices throughout different departments.

Recognition and Incentives: Organizations should honor employees who actively enhance their cybersecurity practices through rewards and recognition. Such practices will encourage employees to adopt proactive security measures.

Example: A manufacturing company can establish a security awareness program that incentivizes employees who report vulnerabilities and attend training sessions to create a vigilant and responsible workplace culture.

Conclusion

Organizations must utilize effective risk assessment and management to shield OT systems from the constantly changing cyber threat landscape. Organizations that understand the specific challenges of OT environments and apply structured risk assessment processes can discover vulnerabilities while evaluating their potential impacts and creating effective risk mitigation strategies.

The chapter detailed essential risk assessment procedures such as asset identification and threat modeling alongside vulnerability assessment and impact analysis before moving to risk evaluation and treatment processes. We analyzed different risk management techniques and highlighted technical controls as well as policy development together with regular audits and community engagement as essential elements to build a security-conscious culture.

Implementing these strategies enables organizations to strengthen their cybersecurity defenses while meeting regulatory standards and preventing attacks on their essential systems. Our discussion in the upcoming chapters will focus on detailed methods for cybersecurity audits along with risk management tools and real-world examples that demonstrate successful strategies. This knowledge will enable organizations to effectively manage OT cybersecurity challenges while developing strong defenses to counteract new threats.

The end of Chapter 5 marks the completion of "The OT Cybersecurity Audit Handbook: Strategies for Success." The upcoming chapters will delve into optimal practices for OT cybersecurity audits along with available tools and techniques for better security measures while showcasing real-world examples where organizations effectively manage their cybersecurity risks. The insights shared here create an actionable framework to improve operational technology security measures against escalating cyber risks.

Chapter 6: Conducting the Audit

Introduction

An Operational Technology (OT) cybersecurity audit serves as a crucial procedure that assesses security measure effectiveness while identifying vulnerabilities and verifying adherence to necessary regulations and standards. Operational Technology audits require assessment of industrial control systems' specific traits and their support for essential processes which differentiate them from traditional IT audits. This chapter serves as an all-inclusive manual to perform an OT cybersecurity audit by detailing audit methodologies and data collection techniques while introducing tools and best practices that facilitate a successful audit process.

Understanding Audit Methodologies

1. Risk-Based Audit Methodology

Overview: The risk-based audit methodology targets risk identification and assessment to direct audit activities depending on their potential organizational impact. Auditors can use this method to distribute resources efficiently while directing their efforts toward areas with high risk.

Key Steps:

Risk Assessment: Begin with an extensive risk assessment to determine which assets are critical and to identify threats, vulnerabilities, and possible impacts. The assessment results will determine which areas the audit will cover and its main points of examination.

Prioritization: Organizations must arrange identified risks by analyzing both their likelihood of occurrence and their potential operational impact. Audits should concentrate their efforts on high-priority risks first.

Example: The audit would focus primarily on vulnerabilities found in PLCs controlling critical machinery because they create safety risks and operational disruptions.

2. Compliance-Based Audit Methodology

Overview: Compliance-based audits determine if organizations follow essential industry regulations and standards. Organizations operating within regulated industries must adopt this methodology because failing to comply with regulations could result in legal penalties and monetary fines.

Key Steps:

Identify Applicable Regulations: Identify the relevant regulations and standards that govern the organization's operations (such as NERC CIP, IEC 62443, ISO/IEC 27001).

Evaluate Compliance: Review the organization's existing policies and controls and evaluate them to ensure they meet the requirements set by identified regulations.

Example: During an audit for NERC CIP compliance an energy company evaluates its cybersecurity policies alongside incident response plans and access controls to verify adherence to standard requirements.

3. Integrated Audit Methodology

Overview: The integrated audit approach merges risk-based analysis with compliance-based evaluation to deliver a full assessment of the organization's cybersecurity framework. This methodology provides a complete overview of security practices together with regulatory compliance.

Key Steps:

Conduct Risk Assessment: The risk assessment process helps to identify essential organizational assets while evaluating possible risks.

Assess Compliance: As part of the audit process, it is necessary to assess how well the organization follows relevant regulations.

Combine Findings: Conduct an analysis of both risk assessment and compliance evaluation results to determine improvement opportunities.

Example: Water treatment plants can implement an integrated audit methodology to assess the risks of their SCADA system alongside environmental regulatory compliance which ensures safety standards and regulatory obligations are fulfilled.

Data Collection Techniques

1. Document Review

Overview: Document review means examining current OT cybersecurity practice documentation. The review must include organizational policies along with established procedures and records from past audits.

Key Actions:

Collect Relevant Documents: Compile security policies and incident response plans along with asset inventories and network diagrams.

Analyze Policies: Assess the performance of current cybersecurity policies and procedures to manage security threats effectively.

Example: An examination of the manufacturing facility's incident response plan may uncover communication protocol deficiencies during cybersecurity incidents which lead to improvement suggestions.

2. Interviews

Overview: Interviews with crucial staff members reveal important information about the organization's cybersecurity practices and cultural approaches. The audit process becomes more robust when auditors engage staff members from multiple departments.

Key Actions:

Identify Key Personnel: Identify the individuals for interviews among IT staff, OT operators and management personnel.

Prepare Questions: The interview questions should explore security practices and incident response while assessing awareness of cybersecurity risks.

Example: Interviews with OT operators can reveal their knowledge of security protocols and their challenges in following them. The gathered information will reveal necessary training programs and policy changes.

3. Technical Assessments

Overview: Technical evaluations of OT systems include vulnerability scanning and penetration testing alongside configuration reviews for security assessment.

Key Actions:

Vulnerability Scanning: Automated tools should be deployed to detect known vulnerabilities within systems and applications. This technique reveals system vulnerabilities which attackers might exploit.

Penetration Testing: Perform controlled penetration tests which replicate cyberattacks to evaluate how well security control's function.

Configuration Reviews: Review system and device settings by comparing them to security standards to detect configuration errors.

Example: The vulnerability assessment on a SCADA system identifies obsolete software that needs updating to address known security threats.

Tools for Conducting OT Cybersecurity Audits

1. Vulnerability Scanners

Overview: Vulnerability scanners provide crucial support to discover potential security vulnerabilities within OT systems. The tools perform automated scans to detect known vulnerabilities along with system misconfigurations and compliance problems.

Key Features:

Automated Scanning: Utilize scanning tools to discover system and application vulnerabilities in a fast and effective manner.

Reporting: Detailed reports should show identified vulnerabilities alongside their severity levels and suggested steps for remediation.

Examples:

Nessus: Nessus serves as a popular vulnerability scanner with extensive scanning functionalities for IT and OT systems. The system detects software vulnerabilities and configuration errors throughout multiple operating systems and applications.

Qualys: The cloud-based solution delivers uninterrupted monitoring and vulnerability scans which allows organizations to keep their security posture current.

Use Case: During a security audit at a power generation facility, the team employed Nessus to examine industrial control systems and found multiple outdated software versions on essential PLCs. The report guides the team on how to allocate patching resources to reduce possible security vulnerabilities.

2. Configuration Management Tools

Overview: Configuration management tools allow organizations to evaluate their operational technology systems' configurations based on defined security standards. Configuration management tools verify that system configurations meet security standards and adhere to best practice guidelines.

Key Features:

Baseline Configuration Assessment: Assess system configurations by comparing them to established security benchmarks to detect any deviations.

Change Tracking: Track configuration changes and notify system administrators about any unauthorized adjustments.

Examples:

CIS-CAT: The Center for Internet Security Configuration Assessment Tool (CIS-CAT) performs evaluations of system configurations using CIS benchmarks to deliver actionable recommendations for system hardening.

Tripwire: The tool maintains surveillance over file integrity and system configurations while issuing alerts when it detects unauthorized modifications that might signal security incidents.

Use Case: The manufacturing company utilizes CIS-CAT to examine SCADA system configurations which revealed multiple departures from established security benchmarks. The assessment enables the organization to apply essential modifications to improve system security.

3. Network Monitoring Tools

Overview: Real-time network traffic monitoring tools assist organizations in OT environments by enabling the detection of security anomalies and potential threats.

Key Features:

Traffic Analysis: Use network traffic analysis to detect unusual patterns which could signal potential cyber threats.

Alerting: Create alerts for suspicious activities and policy violations to facilitate quick incident response actions.

Examples:

SolarWinds: Organizations can utilize this network monitoring tool to gain complete visibility into network performance and security features which help identify unauthorized access attempts and traffic anomalies.

Darktrace: Darktrace provides an AI-powered cybersecurity solution that utilizes machine learning to detect threats instantly and delivers superior protection for OT networks.

Use Case: An energy utility uses Darktrace to survey the traffic of its OT network. The system uncovers anomalous interactions between PLCs and external IPs which leads the security team to investigate to stop data breaches.

4. Incident Response Tools

Overview: Incident response tools enable organizations to manage cybersecurity incidents by supporting detection, response, and recovery from attacks.

Key Features:

Incident Tracking: Establish a single platform that enables organizations to monitor and handle incidents throughout their entire lifecycle from initial detection until final resolution.

Playbooks and Automation: Organizations can streamline their response efforts by providing predefined incident response playbooks together with automation capabilities.

Examples:

Splunk: Splunk functions as a robust SIEM solution that gathers and examines security data from multiple sources to enable organizations to detect security incidents as they happen.

IBM Resilient: IBM Resilient delivers workflows and automation solutions alongside documentation features to enable organizations to handle security incidents with effectiveness.

Use Case: The water treatment facility employs Splunk to oversee its OT systems and rapidly identify suspicious login attempts on its SCADA system. The incident response team activates their response playbook to investigate the source of the login attempts and strengthen security measures to avoid similar future incidents.

Effective Techniques for Performing an OT Cybersecurity Audit

1. Establish Clear Objectives

Importance: The audit team maintains their focus on essential areas because clearly defined objectives shape the audit process.

Actions:

Define Audit Goals: The audit process should include specific targets like verifying adherence to legal standards and identifying security weaknesses while also measuring how well an incident response's function.

Engage Stakeholders: Work with relevant stakeholders to obtain their concerns and objectives input so the audit aligns with organizational priorities.

Example: The manufacturing facility establishes audit objectives to evaluate adherence to IEC 62443 standards and identify safety and operational efficiency vulnerabilities.

2. Ensure Comprehensive Data Collection

Importance: Thorough audits and complete security posture understanding require organizations to collect comprehensive data.

Actions:

Diverse Data Sources: Gather information from multiple sources such as technical assessments along with documentation

, and stakeholder interviews. An approach that covers multiple facets allows for complete consideration of all OT environment elements.

Organize Data Efficiently: Develop an organized system to classify collected data which will make analysis more effective. Data organization involves document categorization while organizing interview notes along with centralized storage for vulnerability scan results.

Example: The audit team gathers information through vulnerability scans while reviewing incident response plans and talking to operators at a chemical processing plant. Their complete strategy helps them discover weaknesses in technical controls and operational procedures.

3. Engage with OT Personnel

Importance: Understanding OT environments' unique challenges and operational needs requires active engagement with operational technology personnel.

Actions:

Conduct Interviews: Plan interviews with essential OT personnel to understand their operational routines, security measures and encountered difficulties. This information provides a pathway to discover potential improvement areas.

Foster Collaboration: The audit team should work together with OT staff during the auditing process. Fostering cooperation between auditors and operational staff builds trust and positions the audit process as a beneficial activity.

Example: During their visit to a manufacturing facility, an audit team will interview control room operators to learn about the practical application of security policies. Operators' feedback might demonstrate current policy impracticalities within operational boundaries which necessitate policy revisions.

4. Prioritize High-Risk Areas

Importance: Directing audit efforts toward high-risk areas enables efficient resource allocation while addressing essential security weaknesses.

Actions:

Utilize Risk Assessments: Use the previous risk assessment to determine which systems and processes represent the highest risk. The audit team can identify and concentrate on the most critical vulnerabilities by prioritizing specific areas during their review process.

Allocate Resources Accordingly: Focus audit resources on high-risk systems but maintain regular evaluations for low-risk areas.

Example: The audit team at an energy company focuses on the SCADA system which controls power generation because of its essential operational role and potential weaknesses while they perform more basic evaluations on less critical systems.

5. Foster Culture of Continuous Improvement

Importance: The creation of a culture that focuses on continuous improvement leads to persistent security awareness together with active defense measures.

Actions:

Share Findings: Post-audit results and recommendations should be distributed to all stakeholders to enhance security awareness and accountability. The establishment of this strategy results in heightened security culture while promoting ongoing enhancements.

Encourage Feedback: Ask employees to provide feedback on both the audit process and its results. The process identifies more improvement opportunities while making employees active participants in security activities.

Example: The audit team presents their findings to facility management and staff following an audit completion and encourages vulnerability discussions along with potential improvement talks. Working together in this way establishes cybersecurity as a collective duty for all involved.

Reporting Audit Findings

1. Structuring the Audit Report

Importance: Audit reports that follow a clear structure deliver transparent communication about findings to stakeholders.

Actions:

Executive Summary: Start the report with an executive summary that presents the objective audit and main findings along with high-level recommendations. Management needs to easily understand this section which presents information in a brief format.

Detailed Findings: Organize detailed findings by category such as compliance and incident response to deliver comprehensive audit results.

Recommendations: Outline practical steps to mitigate discovered vulnerabilities while improving security protocols. Organizations should order recommendations according to the levels of risk and potential consequences they produce.

Example: The water treatment facility audit report features an executive summary that identifies SCADA system vulnerabilities alongside detailed regulatory compliance findings and prioritized remediation recommendations.

2. Communicating Findings to Stakeholders

Importance: When audit findings are communicated effectively, they help stakeholders understand the issues and motivate them to act.

Actions:

Presentation of Findings: Arrange a meeting with essential stakeholders to deliver the audit findings and enable discussion and clarification on identified issues. Key points should be demonstrated through visual materials including charts and graphs.

Encourage Dialogue: The presentation should enable stakeholders to ask questions while the presenter gathers their feedback. Stakeholders will be more likely to support recommendations after having them refined through feedback and discussion.

Example: The audit team shares the results of their audit with the chemical plant management team while explaining identified vulnerabilities and discussing possible operational effects. The team enables management to recognize how critical it is to adopt recommended changes through active discussion and questions.

3. Establishing an Action Plan

Importance: The action plan details necessary steps for addressing audit findings and putting recommendations into operation.

Actions:

Develop Action Items: Formulate a detailed list of action steps based on audit findings that specify required tasks, assign responsibilities and sets completion deadlines.

Assign Responsibilities: Define which personnel will handle each action item to guarantee accountability throughout implementation.

Monitor Progress: Develop a system to track the progress of action items while delivering routine updates to stakeholders. This process keeps remediation efforts moving forward while keeping everyone informed about current progress.

Example: The audit team creates an action plan after reviewing a power generation facility which includes updating aging PLC software and strengthening access control measures together with employee training sessions. Every action item goes to an assigned team member who has a deadline for completion while monthly progress updates take place.

Continuous Improvement Post-Audit

1. Implementing Changes Based on Findings

Importance: The cybersecurity posture of OT systems requires strengthening through the implementation of changes identified in audit findings.

Actions:

Prioritize Remediation Efforts: Focus on addressing high-risk vulnerabilities first. Actions may involve applying critical system patches and improving security controls or making necessary policy revisions.

Engage Relevant Departments: Work closely with IT, OT, and compliance teams to guarantee changes meet operational needs and security standards.

Example: Following an audit that uncovered inadequate access controls for their SCADA system, a manufacturing facility can implement multi-factor authentication for system users to improve security.

2. Conducting Follow-Up Audits

Importance: The process of conducting follow-up audits plays a vital role in evaluating implemented changes and verifying continued adherence to compliance standards.

Actions:

Schedule Regular Audits: Create a regular audit schedule to monitor remediation progress and evaluate the security status of OT systems.

Review Action Plan Effectiveness: Assess whether the implemented changes from the initial audit have successfully reduced the recognized risks.

Example: Six months post-initial audit a water utility should perform a follow-up audit to evaluate security improvements in OT systems and to detect any new vulnerabilities that have surfaced.

3. Maintaining Documentation

Importance: Thorough documentation of audit processes and outcomes enables compliance demonstration and accountability assurance.

Actions:

Document Audit Findings: Keep detailed records of all discovered findings which should cover vulnerabilities as well as compliance issues plus recommendations.

Track Remediation Efforts: Maintain exhaustive documentation of corrective actions for audit findings with specific timelines and assigned responsible parties.

Example: The compliance officer at an energy company creates a centralized database for audit reports together with action plans and remediation documentation to support upcoming audits and regulatory evaluations.

4. Fostering a Culture of Security Awareness

Importance: A robust cybersecurity posture depends on creating a workplace environment where employee security awareness is emphasized and cultivated.

Actions:

Ongoing Training: Employees must receive ongoing training and awareness programs to stay updated on new threats and best practices.

Promote Reporting: Ensure employees feel safe reporting suspicious activities or potential vulnerabilities without fear of retaliation.

Example: The chemical processing plant runs a cybersecurity training program on a regular basis which incorporates simulated phishing exercises to educate employees about identifying and dealing with possible threats.

Conclusion

The OT cybersecurity audit process presents significant complexity yet remains crucial for organizations to assess their security posture while pinpointing vulnerabilities and maintaining regulatory compliance. Organizations that follow a structured methodology while using effective data collection techniques and appropriate tools can acquire valuable insights about their OT security practices.

This chapter presents multiple audit methodologies along with different data collection methods and tools that enhance audit efficiency. Our recommendations for best audit practices feature setting clear objectives along with OT staff engagement and prioritizing high-risk areas before communicating findings clearly.

Following audit completion, the organization should concentrate on applying findings to make improvements while conducting additional audits for validation and sustaining complete records along with promoting security awareness within the organization. Organizations that implement these practices will strengthen their cybersecurity defenses and safeguard critical infrastructure against new threats.

The upcoming sections will present detailed case studies and actual instances of organizations which successfully conducted OT cybersecurity audits alongside risk management strategies. Organizations seeking to fortify their cybersecurity measures can gain valuable guidance from these insights amid a growingly complex threat environment.

We have reached the end of Chapter 6 in "The OT Cybersecurity Audit Handbook: Strategies for Success." Later chapters will analyze actual case studies and prove best practices from organizations that have mastered OT cybersecurity audits to deliver practical insights applicable to readers' operational settings.

Chapter 7: Findings and Reporting in OT Cybersecurity Audits

Introduction

The subsequent essential step after conducting an Operational Technology (OT) environment audit is to examine the results and develop a comprehensive report. This chapter emphasizes why thorough documentation of audit findings matters and explains how to organize reports and deliver outcomes to stakeholders. This section will introduce the best practices for sharing audit findings and recommendations and explore methods to ensure that audit results create significant cybersecurity improvements within the organization.

Importance of Documenting Findings

1. Establishing Accountability

Establishing organizational accountability requires the documentation of audit findings. Maintaining a comprehensive record of vulnerabilities and compliance issues alongside their recommendations enables responsible parties to recognize their duties to address these problems.

2. Supporting Continuous Improvement

Future audits and assessments utilize a well-documented audit report as a foundational reference point. This method enables organizations to measure their remediation progress and assess how well implemented changes function over time.

3. Fostering Transparency

Transparency in reporting promotes trust among stakeholders. The dissemination of audit findings and corrective action plans to stakeholders helps develop a security-focused culture with accountable practices.

4. Ensuring Compliance

Organizations functioning under regulated industry rules must document their audit findings to show they meet necessary regulations and standards. Organizations can use detailed audit records as evidence throughout regulatory evaluations and inspection processes.

Structuring the Audit Report

An organized audit report improves understanding while effectively delivering essential findings. This document details the fundamental parts of an OT cybersecurity audit report.

1. Executive Summary

Overview: The executive summary offers a condensed overview of the audit by presenting the main objectives and summarizing both findings and recommendations. The section must remain brief and understandable for management and stakeholders without technical backgrounds.

Key Components:

Audit Objectives: The audit purpose must be defined with specific objectives that include compliance assessment, vulnerability identification, and incident response capability evaluation.

Key Findings: The summary should present the audit's most crucial findings with an emphasis on high-risk vulnerabilities and critical compliance problems needing urgent action.

Recommendations: Offer a concise summary of top suggestions to rectify detected problems and strengthen organizational cybersecurity defenses.

Example: The audit evaluated the SCADA system's cybersecurity at the water treatment facility against IEC 62443 standards and worked to identify system vulnerabilities. The audit discovered that essential PLCs run outdated software programs along with inadequate access control mechanisms. Our recommendation includes urgent patching of found vulnerabilities along with implementing role-based access controls.

2. Detailed Findings

Overview: The detailed findings section contains an extensive analysis of the audit results sorted by category. This section must present specific vulnerabilities along with compliance matters and potential improvement areas.

Key Components:

Vulnerability Assessments: The audit results should include detailed documentation of all identified vulnerabilities along with their potential effects on operational processes and safety standards.

Compliance Evaluation: Provide a summary of audit findings related to regulatory compliance while highlighting any discrepancies or concerns.

Operational Insights: Gather findings about operational practices as well as employee training and security culture.

Example:

Vulnerabilities:

Outdated PLC Firmware: The audit revealed multiple PLC units operating on obsolete firmware which left them vulnerable to known security exploits. Immediate patching is recommended.

Weak Password Policies: Weak passwords on user accounts have been discovered which creates a higher possibility for unauthorized access.

Compliance Issues:

Incident Response Plan: The organization's incident response plan was obsolete and failed to comply with existing regulatory standards. Review and update are necessary.

Operational Insights:

Employee Awareness: The interviews showed employees lacked understanding of cybersecurity policies which demonstrates the organization needs better training programs.

3. Recommendations

Overview: The recommendations section details practical actions the organization needs to implement to resolve detected security gaps and regulatory compliance problems. Organizations must prioritize their recommendations according to the assessed risk levels and potential consequences.

Key Components:

Actionable Steps: The organization needs to follow detailed practical steps to reduce the risks that have been identified.

Prioritization: Prioritize recommendations by assessing their urgency levels together with their potential operational and safety impacts.

Responsible Parties: Designate individual employees or teams responsible for executing each recommendation throughout the organization.

Example:

Recommendation for Outdated PLC Firmware:

Action: Ensure all critical PLCs receive the latest firmware updates.

Priority: High

Responsible Party: OT Engineering Team

Recommendation for Weak Password Policies:

Action: Introduce a role-based access control system to all user accounts and establish mandatory strong password policies.

Priority: Medium

Responsible Party: IT Security Team

4. Appendices

Overview: The appendices offer supporting documentation and supplementary information that improves the audit report. Stakeholders who want to explore specific audit areas will find this section helpful.

Key Components:

Supporting Documents: The appendices should contain relevant documents including asset inventories, network diagrams, and previous audit reports to back up the findings and recommendations.

Detailed Vulnerability Data: Provide complete vulnerability scan reports which contain individual CVE identifiers along with corresponding risk assessments.

Interview Summaries: Create concise records of all audit interviews with a focus on significant personnel insights and observations.

Glossary of Terms: The report should contain a glossary section that explains all technical terms and acronyms so non-technical stakeholders can understand the content better.

Example: The appendices might include:

Appendix A: Asset Inventory List

Appendix B: Network Diagram of OT Systems

Appendix C: Detailed Vulnerability Scan Results

Appendix D: Summary of Employee Interviews

Appendix E: Glossary of Terms

Communicating Audit Findings to Stakeholders

The proper presentation of audit findings enables stakeholders to grasp the results which leads them to implement the recommendations provided. The section outlines the best practices for presenting findings to different audiences.

1. Tailoring Communication to the Audience

Importance: Stakeholders differ in their technical knowledge and specific areas of interest regarding audit details. Audience-specific communication guarantees that central messages achieve maximum impact.

Actions:

Management: Present management with essential findings and strategic recommendations alongside identified risks. Emphasize the business impact of identified vulnerabilities.

Technical Teams: Provide detailed technical findings and actionable recommendations. When communicating with technical teams, ensure to use precise technical terminology alongside specific data points to enable immediate actions.

Operational Staff: Operational staff must recognize how audit findings and recommendations affect day-to-day operations. Use clear, non-technical language to ensure understanding.

Example: During management presentations the audit team will focus on how SCADA system vulnerabilities could financially impact the organization. When interacting with technical teams they present comprehensive vulnerability information alongside remediation guidance.

2. Using Visual Aids

Importance: Visual tools boost both comprehension and memory of information presented. Visual aids enable users to simplify complicated datasets for easier comprehension.

Actions:

Charts and Graphs: Charts and graphs should be used to represent significant findings which include the count of vulnerabilities categorized by their level of severity and compliance status.

Heat Maps: Through heat maps stakeholders can visually determine the high-risk areas within the OT environment which helps them pinpoint critical focus areas.

Flow Diagrams: Employ flow diagrams as visual tools to represent the incident response procedures and data movement in OT systems while defining respective roles and responsibilities.

Example: The audit team provides a heat map which illustrates locations in the OT environment with the greatest vulnerability density to help management determine resource allocation areas.

3. Encouraging Dialogue

Importance: Dialogue during presentations boosts engagement while giving stakeholders the chance to ask questions and offer feedback.

Actions:

Interactive Presentations: Design your presentations to include time for questions and discussions. Invite stakeholders to express their thoughts and issues.

Follow-Up Discussions: Arrange follow-up meetings to resolve any remaining questions or concerns that surface after presenting initial findings.

Example: The audit lead asks management team members to ask questions and promotes an open conversation regarding the audit findings and suggested recommendations. This method resolves ambiguities while promoting teamwork that advances progress.

Ensuring Meaningful Improvements

An OT cybersecurity audit aims to achieve substantial enhancements in the organization's security framework. This section examines methods to ensure audit findings produce practical and implementable changes.

1. Developing an Action Plan

Importance: The action plan details essential steps for resolving detected vulnerabilities and applying audit suggestions.

Actions:

Define Action Items: Break down recommendations into specific, actionable steps. All action items must specify the tasks to be performed alongside the party responsible and the expected completion timeline.

Prioritize Actions: Classify action items according to their associated risk levels and potential impact. Organizations must tackle high-priority items immediately to quickly reduce the most substantial risks.

Set Deadlines: Each action item needs a clear deadline to promote accountability and sustain remediation progress.

Example: The power generation facility's action plan incorporates several specific items.

Update PLC Firmware:

Action: Ensure all critical PLCs receive the latest firmware updates.

Responsible Party: OT Engineering Team

Deadline: Within 30 days

Implement Role-Based Access Controls:

Action: Implement role-based access management by redesigning controls throughout all OT systems.

Responsible Party: IT Security Team

Deadline: Within 60 days

2. Assigning Responsibilities

Importance: Defining responsibilities creates accountability which then supports the effective execution of the action plan.

Actions:

Identify Key Personnel: Allocate each action item to the appropriate team member or department by considering their expertise and organizational role.

Create Accountability: Make sure that responsible parties acknowledge their duties while recognizing their crucial role in cybersecurity enhancement.

Example: The Human Resources department will receive the responsibility to organize cybersecurity awareness training and ensure employee participation.

3. Monitoring Progress

Importance: The timely completion of remediation efforts depends on consistent monitoring of progress on the action plan.

Actions:

Establish Progress Checkpoints: Set up bi-weekly or monthly meetings to evaluate action item progress and address encountered challenges.

Document Progress: Document progress for each action item by recording completed tasks and ongoing efforts along with any adjustments made to the schedule.

Example: The audit team conducts monthly meetings with stakeholders to assess action item progress through discussions about finished tasks and obstacles that could slow down remediation work.

4. Conducting Follow-Up Audits

Importance: Follow-up audits allow organizations to evaluate whether implemented changes have effectively addressed vulnerabilities and to verify the proper resolution of issues.

Actions:

Schedule Follow-Up Audits: Set up follow-up audits at consistent intervals such as every six months to one year following the initial audit to review both the existing security environment and the progress on action items.

Reassess Vulnerabilities: Review discovered earlier vulnerabilities to check if they have been resolved and to detect any new vulnerabilities that have appeared.

Example: Six months following the initial audit a water utility conducts a second audit to evaluate the implementation of suggested changes. The audit results show better access controls but reveal new remote access vulnerabilities needing attention.

5. Updating Policies and Procedures

Importance: The continuous updating of policies and procedures maintains their effectiveness and relevance against new threats and vulnerabilities.

Actions:

Review Security Policies: Once the audit concludes, it is crucial to revisit and modify security policies to include new insights gained from the audit alongside technological advancements and shifting regulatory demands.

Incorporate Best Practices: Operational procedures and guidelines must include the best practices discovered through the audit process.

Example: The organization updated its policies by adding detailed communication procedures for cybersecurity incidents following an audit that revealed weaknesses in its incident response plan and assigned specific responsibilities for incident response.

6. Enhancing Training and Awareness Programs

Importance: The success of cybersecurity strategies hinges on employee training and awareness because human behavior frequently leads to security incidents.

Actions:

Develop Training Programs: Audit findings should guide the creation or improvement of training programs that teach cybersecurity best practices and incident reporting while increasing awareness of potential threats.

Conduct Regular Training Sessions: Regular training sessions should be set up to keep employees updated on emerging threats and organizational security policies.

Example: The manufacturing facility conducts a quarterly training program which features phishing simulations and insider threat recognition workshops to empower employees in supporting organizational cybersecurity initiatives.

Conclusion

The findings and reporting phase serve as a vital component of the entire OT cybersecurity audit procedure. Organizations need to document findings properly while structuring audit reports and communicating results to stakeholders to achieve meaningful cybersecurity improvements.

This chapter explains why audit findings need proper documentation and describes what makes up an effective audit report through sections such as the executive summary and detailed findings along with recommendations and appendices. We went over the best practices for delivering findings to different stakeholders while guaranteeing clear communication and active involvement.

Organizations need to establish explicit action plans and assign responsibilities while monitoring progress and conducting follow-up audits to turn audit findings into actionable changes and they should update policies and training programs. Organizations that implement these measures can resolve recognized weaknesses while nurturing continuous improvement and reinforcing their cybersecurity posture against new threats.

The upcoming chapters will present organizational case studies that detail successful OT cybersecurity audits and the subsequent learnings from those experiences. Organizations that want to improve their cybersecurity efforts in operational technology will find practical insights and guidance through these real-world examples.

Chapter 7 from "The OT Cybersecurity Audit Handbook: Strategies for Success" has reached its conclusion. Future chapters will analyze case studies and real-world examples from businesses that have successfully managed OT cybersecurity audit complexities while supplying readers with actionable strategies for their own environments.

Chapter 8: Organizations must create an action plan to address findings from OT cybersecurity audits.

Introduction

Organizations obtain extensive data on their security posture, vulnerabilities and regulatory compliance following an Operational Technology (OT) cybersecurity audit. The audit produces meaningful results only through implementing actions that correct the discovered problems. This chapter demonstrates how to create an effective action plan using the results from cybersecurity audits. This section covers essential elements that make an action plan successful while also detailing how to prioritize remediation steps and outlining effective methods for implementation and monitoring.

Importance of an Action Plan

1. Translating Findings into Action

An action plan functions as a link between audit findings and actual cybersecurity advancements. The action plan converts academic insights into concrete measures which resolve security weaknesses and improve protective strategies.

2. Prioritization of Resources

Operational Technology environments typically operate with restricted resources. Organizations can use an action plan to focus their remediation resources on the highest-risk vulnerabilities first.

3. Accountability and Ownership

Specific individuals or teams receive assigned responsibilities through defined action items which create accountability. This clear understanding guarantees that everyone knows their part in enhancing the organization's cybersecurity defense.

4. Tracking Progress

An action plan establishes a tracking framework for monitoring remediation progress. Organizations can track implementation progress and make necessary adjustments to guarantee that all action items are completed successfully.

5. Continuous Improvement

Organizations can assess their remediation progress by maintaining records of steps taken after audit findings reveal issues. Ongoing cybersecurity enhancements result from this persistent assessment process.

Components of an Effective Action Plan

A successful action plan must contain multiple essential elements to tackle audit findings in a thorough and streamlined manner.

1. Clear Objectives

Overview: The plan requires each action item to possess specific objectives that match the identified audit findings. Objectives need to be specific, measurable, achievable, relevant, and time-bound according to SMART criteria.

Example:

Objective: All outdated PLC firmware should be updated to their most recent versions.

Specific: Locate outdated firmware versions on PLCs and apply necessary patches to update them.

Measurable: Track the number of PLCs updated.

Achievable: Allocate sufficient resources to complete the task successfully.

Relevant: Address critical vulnerability.

Time-bound: Complete the updates within 30 days.

2. Action Items

Overview: Action items represent the exact tasks required to accomplish the outlined objectives. All items need to be presented in clear language and divided into practical tasks.

Example:

Action Item: Conduct firmware update on PLCs.

Tasks:

Identify all PLCs with outdated firmware.

Access and download the newest firmware releases directly from the manufacturer's official website.

Schedule downtime to apply the updates.

Test the systems post-update to ensure functionality.

3. Assigned Responsibilities

Overview: Each action item requires designated responsibility to ensure accountability. Every task needs to be assigned to either an individual or a team.

Example:

Action Item: Update PLC firmware.

Responsible Party: OT Engineering Team

Support: IT Department (for network support during updates)

4. Timeline

Overview: Creating specific timelines for action items sets clear expectations and guarantees they will be finished on time. The timeline needs to reflect task complexity and remain achievable.

Example:

Action Item: Conduct firmware update on PLCs.

Timeline:

Start Date: [Date]

End Date: [Date]

Review Date: [Date for follow-up assessment]

5. Resource Requirements

Overview: Successful execution depends on determining the essential resources which include personnel, tools, and budget requirements.

Example:

Action Item: Update PLC firmware.

Required Resources:

Access to PLCs for updates

Firmware update tools

Technical support from the IT department

6. Success Criteria

Overview: Create benchmarks to evaluate the effectiveness of every action item implemented. The evaluation process determines if the action successfully reduced the identified risks.

Example:

Action Item: Update PLC firmware.

Success Criteria:

All PLCs are updated within the timeline.

During the update process operational disruptions were not reported.

A post-update audit verified the firmware versions.

Prioritizing Remediation Efforts

Organizations need to prioritize their remediation tasks properly because different vulnerabilities carry varying levels of risk. This section discusses strategies for prioritization.

1. Risk Assessment

Overview: Use the audit risk assessment results to establish remediation priorities according to the vulnerabilities' severity levels.

Actions:

1. Risk Assessment (continued)

Categorize Vulnerabilities: Group vulnerabilities into critical, high, medium, and low categories by evaluating their potential impact and the likelihood they will be exploited. Remediation efforts need to be prioritized according to the established vulnerability categories.

Example: During an industrial control system audit vulnerabilities can be classified into different categories.

Critical: PLCs with unpatched vulnerabilities may enable unauthorized control over industrial machinery.

High: The SCADA system faces potential unauthorized access because of insufficient access control safeguards.

Medium: Non-critical applications with outdated software present potential organizational risks even though they do not affect safety.

Low: Configuration problems which present no immediate danger.

2. Compliance Requirements

Overview: The organization must factor in regulatory compliance requirements to establish remediation priorities. Some vulnerabilities require prompt action to stay compliant while other vulnerabilities can wait.

Actions:

Identify Regulatory Implications: Examine relevant regulations and standards to identify which vulnerabilities need attention for compliance. Compliance standards such as IEC 62443 and NERC CIP along with ISO/IEC 27001 represent possible requirements to address.

Example: Energy companies should focus on fixing their incident response plan vulnerabilities to meet NERC CIP standards since these standards require a strong incident response process.

3. Operational Impact

Overview: Assess the potential effects of vulnerabilities on business operations and employee safety. Remediation activities should focus on vulnerabilities with the potential to disrupt essential processes and compromise employee safety.

Actions:

Assess Operational Dependencies: Determine which systems and processes would face the most significant impact from the exploitation of vulnerability. Focus resources on vulnerabilities that have the potential to cause major operational disruptions.

Example: SCADA system vulnerabilities controlling production lines would take precedence over administrative system weaknesses in manufacturing facilities because they have direct impacts on production and safety.

4. Resource Availability

Overview: Prioritization of remediation efforts should consider both personnel availability and budget constraints. Critical vulnerabilities might require temporary deferral when adequate resources are unavailable for immediate resolution.

Actions:

Evaluate Resource Constraints: Examine the current availability of resources needed for remediation such as budget and tools before establishing a priority list.

Example: When specialized training or tools necessary to fix a critical vulnerability are unavailable immediately, organizations should concentrate on mitigating other high-risk vulnerabilities that they can manage with current resources.

Implementation of the Action Plan

After developing and prioritizing the action plan the organization should begin effective implementation of the identified actions. This section provides the best practices that ensure successful implementation.

1. Communication with Stakeholders

Overview: During the implementation stage effective communication with stakeholders remains crucial. It is crucial for all team members to know their assigned duties together with the set timelines and understand why their actions matter.

Actions:

Kick-Off Meetings: Hold kick-off meetings with relevant teams to go over the action plan while reviewing responsibilities and establishing collaborative expectations.

Regular Updates: Keep stakeholders informed about progress, developments and any alterations to timelines or responsibilities.

Example: The project manager arranges a kick-off meeting to review the PLC firmware update action plan with OT engineering team members and both IT support staff and management. The meeting establishes both the project timeline and clarifies team roles.

2. Resource Allocation

Overview: Each action item should receive sufficient resources. Successful implementation demands appropriate personnel, financial resources and necessary tools.

Actions:

Assess Resource Needs: Verify the availability of essential resources like tools and training before beginning the implementation process.

Allocate Budget: Confirm that the budget allocation for remediation activities has received official approval.

Example: The OT engineering team verifies their access to both the latest PLC firmware versions and essential update tools before proceeding with their firmware update task. The team ensures time is set aside for testing following the updates.

3. Training and Awareness

Overview: Personnel need training and awareness programs to fully understand new policies and technologies introduced during remediation.

Actions:

Conduct Training Sessions: Set up training programs for appropriate staff to introduce them to new security measures and tools.

Promote Security Awareness: Promote cybersecurity best practices through constant training and resource provision to build a security-conscious culture.

Example: The IT security team holds training sessions for all employees to help them understand the new access control policies and the importance of maintaining strong passwords after implementing these measures.

4. Monitoring and Evaluation

Overview: Effective execution of an action plan alongside risk mitigation requires ongoing monitoring and evaluation of implementation efforts.

Actions:

Monitor Progress: Project management tools enable teams to monitor action item statuses while confirming that timelines stay on track and obstacles are resolved.

Example: A project manager sets up a dashboard through a project management tool to monitor PLC firmware updates. The project management system assigns a status to each update task while visually displaying deadlines so the team can detect any schedule delays immediately.

Conduct Regular Reviews: Arrange regular evaluations to assess how well the implemented actions perform. The implemented process guarantees that task completion goes hand in hand with the achievement of organizational goals.

Example: The audit team holds monthly meetings with the OT engineering team to evaluate action item statuses and determine if risk mitigation from audit findings has been successful.

5. Adjusting the Action Plan

Overview: The action plan might require revisions as implementation proceeds to address emerging information and unexpected situations or shifting conditions.

Actions:

Be Flexible: Remain flexible to update timelines, responsibilities, and action items according to project needs. Ongoing evaluations and stakeholder feedback should guide necessary adjustments.

Example: The organization must prioritize and adjust other action items if a critical SCADA system vulnerability emerges during action plan implementation.

Document Changes: Maintain documentation of all modifications to the action plan and explain the reasons for each change. This documentation provides transparency and accountability.

Example: The project manager keeps an updated log which tracks all changes to the action plan including deadline modifications and newly identified vulnerabilities and provides explanations for each change.

Monitoring and Reporting Progress

Organizations need to actively monitor progress while providing regular updates on the status of remediation efforts as soon as the action plan begins. The continuous evaluation process plays a key role in maintaining accountability while supporting ongoing improvement efforts.

1. Establishing Key Performance Indicators (KPIs)

Overview: Key Performance Indicators (KPIs) serve as essential tools to assess the effectiveness of the action plan and to monitor advancements towards remediation benchmarks.

Actions:

Define Relevant KPIs: The action items require specific KPIs which track remediation progress through metrics like vulnerabilities addressed, duration of update completion, and compliance score enhancements.

Example: The action item to update PLC firmware can be measured through relevant KPIs such as:

The proportion of PLCs that received updates within the designated schedule.

Tracking reported incident numbers about firmware vulnerabilities before and after update implementations.

Regularly Review KPIs: Carry out regular checks on KPIs to track advancements and pinpoint areas needing extra attention or resources.

Example: The security team conducts bi-weekly assessments of PLC update percentages and modifies resource allocation or schedule timelines according to the progress updates received.

2. Reporting on Progress

Overview: Consistent updates on the action plan's status ensure transparency and provide stakeholders with information about remediation progress.

Actions:

Create Progress Reports: Periodic progress reports should be developed to display the status of action items by documenting completed tasks along with ongoing efforts and any challenges that arose.

Example: Progress reports issued monthly will show that 75% of vulnerabilities have been fixed and detail any access control implementation delays.

Share Results with Stakeholders: Provide relevant stakeholders such as management and IT and OT teams with progress reports to keep everyone updated on current statuses and required adjustments.

Example: The audit team delivers the progress report to executive leadership while offering insights about remediation successes and needed focus areas.

3. Conducting Follow-up Assessments

Overview: Regular follow-up assessments help determine if implemented changes worked well and confirm that vulnerabilities have been properly handled.

Actions:

Schedule Follow-up Audits: Establish recurring audit schedules to evaluate your security posture and track action item progress 6 months to 1 year after your initial audit.

Example: A water treatment facility arranges a follow-up audit six months post their initial audit to determine if SCADA system security enhancements are effective.

Reassess Vulnerabilities: Assessments during follow-up evaluations should reexamine previously identified vulnerabilities to verify their mitigation status and identify any new vulnerabilities that have been developed.

Example: The follow-up audit shows improved access control but highlights new vulnerabilities with remote access tools that require attention.

Continuous Improvement and Lessons Learned

Implementing the action plan starts an ongoing cycle of enhancements. Organizations must evaluate their entire auditing process to learn from past experiences and adjust to improve future audits.

1. Conducting a Post-Implementation Review

Overview: Post-implementation reviews evaluate remediation efforts' success and pull key insights from the overall process.

Actions:

Gather Feedback: The action plan implementation requires feedback collection from IT, OT teams and management personnel. The feedback received from implementation teams helps identify successful strategies and the difficulties faced during the implementation phase.

Example: Once the audit action items have been finished the project manager calls together key stakeholders to review the results. The team discussed both successful outcomes like the PLC firmware update and encountered challenges including training program delays during the meeting.

Document Lessons Learned: Write a report that captures the knowledge gained during the implementation process. Documentation must cover both successful outcomes and improvement areas which future audits and action plans can use as references.

Example: The post-implementation review shows that technical updates proceeded without issue but revealed that the employee training program did not meet expected effectiveness standards. This understanding drives the choice to improve the future training approaches.

2. Updating Policies and Procedures

Overview: Organizations need to continuously update their cybersecurity policies and procedures through regular audits and lessons learned.

Actions:

Review Existing Policies: Analyze existing policies through the lens of audit outcomes and post-implementation evaluations. Locate any outdated procedures that require updates during the review process.

Example: The organization uncovers through their audit results that their incident response plan lacks integration of insights gained from recent incidents. The organization updates the plan to integrate new protocols which will address emerging threats effectively.

Incorporate Best Practices: The organization should integrate the best practices discovered during both audit and implementation stages into its policies to improve cybersecurity practices.

Example: The organization implements a policy mandating regular phishing simulation exercises within the employee training program due to feedback revealing employees require additional practice to recognize phishing attacks.

3. Strengthening the Security Culture

Overview: The development of a robust security culture is crucial for maintaining cybersecurity as an organizational priority. Employee engagement together with better adherence to security protocols will improve when this cultural transformation takes place.

Actions:

Promote Awareness Programs: Establish continuous security awareness programs that actively involve employees and drive them to participate in cybersecurity protection efforts.

Example: Employees receive a monthly cybersecurity newsletter from the organization which outlines current threats and provides safety tips along with employee success stories of reported suspicious activities.

Encourage Reporting and Feedback: Develop a workplace atmosphere where employees can report security incidents and vulnerabilities without worrying about retaliation. The system enables organizations to recognize potential threats sooner.

Example: Employees can anonymously report their concerns through the organization's "Report a Threat" program. The organization strengthens its security program by conducting training sessions and internal communication materials that emphasize vigilance.

4. Engaging in Ongoing Training

Overview: Employees need continuous training to stay updated on cybersecurity risks and best practices. The organization's security posture becomes stronger through consistent training sessions.

Actions:

Implement Regular Training Sessions: Organize regular cybersecurity training sessions to teach employees about phishing awareness, incident response procedures, and secure usage of OT systems.

Example: The manufacturing facility organizes quarterly training which features practical exercises like simulated phishing attacks to strengthen learning and prepare employees to handle threats effectively.

Tailor Training to Roles: Create role-specific training programs that teach employees their cybersecurity responsibilities based on their position within the organization.

Example: The organization offers targeted training to OT personnel emphasizing how to protect industrial control systems and understand cybersecurity's effects on operational safety.

Conclusion

Creating an action plan after an OT cybersecurity audit represents an essential step to transform identified findings into significant advancements. A successful action plan features distinct objectives and detailed action steps along with designated responsibilities and timelines while including resource needs and performance indicators.

Organizations achieve better protection by addressing critical vulnerabilities first through remediation efforts which prioritize risk assessment results alongside compliance requirements and operational impacts and resource availability. The action plan implementation requires effective communication along with proper resource allocation and training while monitoring progress.

Organizations must commit to ongoing improvement to sustain their cybersecurity defenses. This process requires post-implementation reviews together with updated policies and procedures alongside strengthened security culture and ongoing training.

Organizations that implement these best practices can both resolve audit-detected vulnerabilities and build a continuous improvement culture which improves their defense mechanisms against new cyber threats.

The subsequent chapters will present actual examples of organizations that developed and executed action plans informed by their audit reports. The upcoming case studies deliver hands-on guidance to help organizations boost their cybersecurity defenses within operational technology landscapes.

We have reached the end of Chapter 8 in "The OT Cybersecurity Audit Handbook: Strategies for Success." Upcoming chapters will analyze detailed case studies alongside real-world examples from organizations that have mastered OT cybersecurity audits to give readers practical strategies they can implement in their own settings.

Chapter 9: Continuous Improvement and Monitoring in OT Cybersecurity

Introduction

The field of Operational Technology (OT) cybersecurity requires continuous improvement and monitoring because it is evolving so quickly that these practices become critical. Security practices of organizations need to evolve as cyber threats demonstrate rising levels of sophistication. This chapter explores the foundational principles for continuous improvement and monitoring as well as best practices to develop a sustainable cybersecurity program for OT environments. Our exploration will cover assessment methods for security performance along with monitoring tools and approaches to develop security awareness culture.

The Need for Continuous Improvement

1. Evolving Threat Landscape

The cyber threat landscape evolves continuously because of advancements in technology alongside the inventive methods used by malicious actors. Organizations need to consistently evaluate their security systems while improving them because of newly discovered vulnerabilities and the exploitation of existing ones.

Example: Organizations have started reassessing their incident response strategies and preparedness levels because of the increasing ransomware attacks on critical infrastructure.

2. Regulatory Compliance

Maintaining adherence to industry regulations and standards demands continuous efforts for compliance. Through regular assessments organizations can keep up with regulatory changes and prevent any resulting penalties.

Example: Organizations subject to NERC CIP standards need to routinely examine their cybersecurity practices to maintain compliance as regulations evolve to address new threats.

3. Organizational Resilience

The practice of continuous improvement strengthens organizational resilience through its capacity to help organizations respond to technological developments and evolving regulatory requirements and threat environments. Maintaining operational continuity requires adaptability during cyber incidents.

Example: Utility companies which consistently improve their response plans with insights from previous incidents develop stronger defenses against upcoming threats.

Establishing a Continuous Improvement Framework

Organizations need to implement a systematic framework to support ongoing cybersecurity improvement that integrates continuous assessments and feedback mechanisms with strategic enhancement measures.

1. Regular Security Assessments

Overview: Organizations need to perform regular security assessments to discover weaknesses and review their current control measures' performance.

Actions:

Scheduled Audits: Organizations should schedule regular cybersecurity audits which perform evaluations of policy compliance and regulatory adherence while identifying security gaps and testing control effectiveness.

Example: Organizations should perform yearly OT cybersecurity audits and add quarterly vulnerability assessments to keep their security posture current.

Penetration Testing: Use penetration testing to recreate cyberattacks and assess how well organizational defenses stand up to actual threats.

Example: External experts perform penetration tests on a manufacturing facility's SCADA systems and identify weaknesses in access controls that require mitigation.

2. Feedback Mechanisms

Overview: Through feedback mechanisms organizations acquire stakeholder insights to modify their policies and practices effectively.

Actions:

Employee Surveys: Organizations should conduct employee surveys to evaluate cybersecurity awareness levels and collect feedback on training effectiveness.

Example: Surveys enable organizations to assess how effective their cybersecurity training programs are and identify specific areas where employees lack confidence.

Incident Reviews: Perform a post-mortem analysis following any security incident to understand the failures and successes and identify improvement opportunities.

Example: The organization holds a review meeting after a phishing attack resulted in unauthorized access to examine the incident and seek improvements for email security protocols and staff training methods.

3. Continuous Training and Awareness Programs

Overview: Continuous training programs play an essential role in educating employees about new threats while strengthening their knowledge of best practices.

Actions:

Regular Training Sessions: Organize regular training sessions that focus on the newest cybersecurity threats and best practices.

Example: A healthcare organization conducts training sessions every quarter to teach staff how to identify phishing attempts so they can protect themselves from social engineering attacks.

Security Awareness Campaigns: Establish campaigns that build a strong security awareness culture throughout the organization.

Example: During their "Cybersecurity Month" campaign a manufacturing company conducts workshops and distributes both posters and emails that focus on best practices and current cybersecurity threats.

Monitoring in OT Environments

Continuous monitoring remains an essential element of cybersecurity strategies within operational technology settings. Organizations maintain security posture visibility through continuous monitoring which helps them detect anomalies and respond to incidents as they happen.

1. Importance of Monitoring

Overview: Real-time monitoring systems enable organizations to maintain constant visibility in their OT environments which allows them to detect potential threats and respond to them proactively.

Actions:

Detecting Anomalies: Monitoring tools detect abnormal network traffic patterns and system behavior which may signal a potential security incident.

Example: The OT monitoring system identifies irregular communication between PLCs and external systems which prompts alert notifications for detailed examination.

Incident Response Capabilities: Real-time monitoring strengthens incident response capabilities through the provision of immediate threat information.

Example: A monitoring solution detects unauthorized access attempts to SCADA systems and enables the security team to take swift action against the threat.

2. Tools for Monitoring OT Environments

Multiple monitoring tools designed for OT environments provide specialized functionalities that enable anomaly detection and cybersecurity improvement. The effectiveness of monitoring efforts and incident responses depends upon choosing appropriate tools.

a. Security Information and Event Management (SIEM) Solutions

Overview: SIEM solutions analyze security data from multiple organizational sources to deliver real-time alerts and insights about potential security incidents.

Key Features:

Log Management: Analyze and aggregate logs from OT systems alongside network and application data to discover abnormal patterns.

Real-Time Alerts: Create alerts according to predefined rules and thresholds to enable security teams to react swiftly to security incidents.

Examples:

Splunk: Splunk represents a widely used SIEM platform through which OT system monitoring becomes possible after logging ingestion from multiple sources for complete analysis and alert generation.

IBM QRadar: This SIEM application offers sophisticated analytics and machine learning functions to identify irregularities within OT environments.

Use Case: The manufacturing facility deploys Splunk to collect and integrate logs from both its SCADA system and network equipment. The SIEM solution detects unusual login activity from a new IP source which leads to an investigation of possible unauthorized access.

b. Network Monitoring Tools

Overview: Network monitoring tools analyze network traffic in real time to enable organizations to identify anomalies and security threats within OT environments.

Key Features:

Traffic Analysis: Track network traffic patterns to detect abnormal behavior which might signal a cyber threat.

Protocol Analysis: Examine OT system communication protocols to confirm their behavior matches expected patterns.

Examples:

SolarWinds Network Performance Monitor: The software enables organizations to track network performance and security to spot unusual activity within OT communications.

Darktrace: The Darktrace platform uses machine learning algorithms to detect threats as they happen by analyzing what normal behavior looks like.

Use Case: A Darktrace system monitors network traffic in the OT environment of an energy company. The AI identifies abnormal communication patterns between a PLC and external servers which leads to an investigation discovering a possible malware infection.

c. Intrusion Detection and Prevention Systems (IDPS)

Overview: IDPS systems track network and system activities to identify malicious actions and policy breaches and generate alerts or initiate responses using established rules.

Key Features:

Signature-Based Detection: Identify known threats based on predefined signatures.

Anomaly-Based Detection: The detection of atypical behavior patterns can reveal the presence of previously unidentified threats.

Examples:

Snort: Snort functions as an open-source intrusion detection system that administrators can configure to watch network traffic for suspicious behaviors affecting OT settings.

Cisco Firepower: This security solution provides intrusion prevention features specifically designed for industrial network environments.

Use Case: The pharmaceutical company uses Snort for monitoring its OT network operations. Security teams receive notifications from the system when unusual network traffic patterns emerge that suggest potential breach attempts enabling fast investigation response.

d. Endpoint Protection Solutions

Overview: Endpoint protection solutions defend OT network devices including PLCs, HMIs and sensors by recognizing and reacting to threats directly on the devices.

Key Features:

Malware Detection: Detect and protect OT devices from malware attacks.

Device Control: Maintain control over connected device security through continuous monitoring.

Examples:

Carbon Black: The endpoint protection platform delivers superior detection and response features to protect OT devices from potential threats.

McAfee Total Protection for Endpoint: McAfee Total Protection for Endpoint delivers full security coverage for network endpoints as well as those used in OT settings.

Use Case: The water treatment plant uses Carbon Black to track its PLCs and HMIs. The platform identifies a malware variant targeting PLC firmware vulnerability which enables the security team to implement preventive measures before any harm occurs.

3. Establishing a Monitoring Strategy

Organizations need to create a strong monitoring strategy for OT environments which defines both the goals and processes as well as the monitoring tools to be used.

a. Define Monitoring Objectives

Overview: Set explicit monitoring objectives to maintain consistency with both company goals and regulatory standards.

Actions:

Identify Key Risks: The monitoring efforts need to focus on main risks including unauthorized access incidents, data breaches, and operational disruptions.

Set Performance Metrics: Establish performance measures for assessing the success of monitoring activities.

Example: The organization aims to reduce security alert response time by 50% during the upcoming year to improve its real-time threat mitigation capabilities.

b. Select Appropriate Tools

Overview: Select monitoring tools that match both the organization's specific requirements and its OT environment's distinct features.

Actions:

Evaluate Compatibility: It is essential to choose monitoring tools that work well with current OT systems while also being capable of tracking necessary protocols and technologies.

Consider Integration: Assess how effectively the tools work together with other security solutions like SIEM systems and incident response platforms.

Example: A manufacturing plant examines different network monitoring tools to choose one that integrates smoothly with its current SIEM solution for centralized security event visibility and analysis.

c. Develop Monitoring Policies and Procedures

Overview: Develop precise policies and procedures for monitoring operations defining roles and responsibilities together with escalation processes and response protocols.

Actions:

Define Roles and Responsibilities: Identify the personnel accountable for monitoring system operations and analyzing alerts as well as handling incident responses. It is essential for team members to comprehend their specific functions within the monitoring process.

Example: The utility company's cybersecurity team defines its monitoring policy by assigning specific analysts to track SIEM alerts and launch investigations when needed.

Establish Escalation Procedures: Design an explicit escalation process for incidents that monitoring systems detect. The process requires establishing alert thresholds for management notifications and coordinating response actions.

Example: The organization establishes an escalation protocol which mandates the security director be notified right away about critical alerts pertaining to unauthorized access attempts on OT systems.

d. Implement Continuous Monitoring

Overview: Continuous monitoring means organizations evaluate security events and anomalies as they occur to enable quick responses to new threats.

Actions:

Configure Alerting Mechanisms: Configure monitoring tools to generate alerts for critical events that include unauthorized access attempts and unusual network traffic or deviations from standard baselines.

Example: The SIEM system at a chemical processing plant generates real-time alerts for security personnel upon detecting unusual activity in the SCADA system to enable quick investigations.

Conduct Regular Reviews: Routine examination of monitoring logs and alerts helps discover patterns while evaluating monitoring success and improves operational processes when necessary.

Example: The security team at an energy company conducts weekly review meetings to analyze monitoring data and discuss significant alerts before evaluating the operational technology security environment's health.

Fostering a Culture of Security Awareness

For continuous improvement and monitoring efforts to function effectively organizations need to establish a robust security awareness culture among their entire staff. Adopting this cultural change can substantially strengthen the organization's security posture.

1. Leadership Commitment

Overview: Leadership holds a fundamental position in establishing a culture of security awareness throughout the organization. Organizational members understand the significance of security when their leaders focus on cybersecurity.

Actions:

Set the Tone: Leadership must consistently communicate both cybersecurity importance and their dedication to safeguarding

OT systems. Leadership can achieve this by organizing meetings and disseminating information through newsletters and internal communications.

Example: At a company-wide meeting the CEO of a manufacturing firm informs staff about the critical role cybersecurity plays in safeguarding both operational functions and the organization's reputation.

Allocate Resources: Adequate resources must be allocated to support security training and awareness programs. Leadership needs to endorse programs that boost employee participation in cybersecurity activities.

Example: The organization invests in cybersecurity training programs through budget allocation because they consider employee awareness to be an essential part of their security strategy.

2. Employee Involvement

Overview: When employees participate in cybersecurity initiatives, they develop ownership and responsibility toward security maintenance.

Actions:

Find out how employees view their organization's security practices.

Phishing Simulations: Analyze results from phishing simulations to determine the number of employees who successfully identify and report phishing attempts. The data gathered reveals which areas require additional training.

Example: The organization examined the results of their phishing simulation to discover that 30% of their employees were engaged with the fake phishing link. The results suggest organizations should implement more specific training to help employees identify phishing attempts.

This section presents real-world examples of organizations implementing ongoing improvement practices in OT cybersecurity systems.

This chapter will demonstrate its concepts through real-world examples of organizations that implemented continuous improvement and monitoring in their OT cybersecurity programs.

Case Study 1: A Power Generation Company

Background: The power generation company encountered an escalation of cyber threats aimed at its SCADA systems. The cybersecurity audit revealed multiple vulnerabilities at the organization such as obsolete software and inadequate employee training.

Implementation of Continuous Improvement:

Regular Security Assessments: The organization implemented yearly cybersecurity audits along with quarterly vulnerability assessments as part of its strategy to protect against new threats.

Employee Training Programs: The organization created an extensive training program which covered phishing awareness skills and incident response methods while teaching employees safe practices for operating OT systems.

Monitoring and Alerts: The organization deployed a SIEM solution which collected SCADA system logs and sent immediate alerts whenever unusual activities were detected.

Results:

Every vulnerability found during the audit was patched by the organization within a three-month timeframe.

Employee understanding of cyber threats improved dramatically according to their better performance results in phishing simulations.

The monitoring system identified an attempted cyberattack and enabled the company to neutralize the threat before operations were affected.

Case Study 2: A Water Treatment Facility

Background: The water treatment facility acknowledged the necessity for stronger cybersecurity protection after multiple attacks targeted critical infrastructure throughout their industry. The audit identified security vulnerabilities in access control systems and incident response strategies.

Implementation of Continuous Improvement:

Incident Response Plan Update: The facility revised its incident response plan to detail cyber incident procedures and conducted training for all employees on the updated protocols.

Implementation of Monitoring Tools: Network monitoring tools were implemented by the organization to track OT device communications and send alerts about anomalies to the security team.

Security Awareness Campaigns: The facility initiated a security awareness campaign which used posters and newsletters as well as interactive training sessions to teach employees about cybersecurity practices.

Results:

The facility demonstrated improved preparedness by successfully containing a cyber incident involving unauthorized access attempts after implementing their updated incident response plan.

The facility used monitoring tools to gain actionable insights which helped them proactively find and resolve security vulnerabilities.

The substantial rise in employee participation in security awareness programs resulted in the development of a more security-aware organizational culture.

Case Study 3: A Chemical Manufacturing Plant

Background: The chemical manufacturing plant worried about how cyber-attacks might affect its production operations. Significant cybersecurity practice gaps were discovered through an audit with deficiencies found in employee training and the monitoring of OT systems.

Implementation of Continuous Improvement:

Comprehensive Training Program: The manufacturing plant created a strong training curriculum with regular training on cybersecurity best practices along with incident reporting techniques and instilling the security-first mindset.

Deployment of IDPS: The organization deployed an Intrusion Detection and Prevention System (IDPS) which continuously monitors network traffic to detect possible threats as they occur.

Post-Implementation Reviews: Following each major security initiative the organization performed post-implementation reviews to evaluate its effectiveness and collect feedback for future improvements.

Results:

Employee understanding of cybersecurity risks expanded through an extensive training program that resulted in decreased security incidents.

Multiple unauthorized access attempts detected by the IDPS enabled the security team to react swiftly and reduce potential dangers.

The organization implemented continuous improvement practices by actively gathering employee feedback to enhance security procedures.

Key Takeaways for Continuous Improvement and Monitoring

Adopt a Proactive Approach: To remain ahead of emerging threats organizations need to establish a priority for proactive steps which include continuous monitoring and regular evaluations.

Foster a Culture of Security: Promoting cybersecurity awareness and involving employees in security initiatives creates a protective culture that strengthens organizational resilience.

Utilize Technology Effectively: Organizations need to implement appropriate monitoring and incident response tools to ensure visibility in the OT environment and enable rapid threat response.

Document and Evaluate: Documenting all outcomes and activities enables organizations to sustain ongoing improvement and ensure accountability.

Remain Agile: Organizations must stay flexible about their cybersecurity strategies as they encounter new threats and technological changes along with evolving regulatory requirements.

Conclusion

A strong OT cybersecurity strategy requires ongoing enhancement, paired with vigilant monitoring practices. Organizations facing dynamic threat environments should establish regular security posture evaluations while promoting employee cybersecurity awareness and implementing technological solutions for improved monitoring.

The chapter explains why organizations need continuous improvement while establishing effective monitoring strategies and building a security culture based on employees' perceptions.

Phishing Simulations: Monitor phishing simulation results to determine the number of employees who identify and report phishing emails. The data gathered reveals which areas require additional training.

Example: The organization analyzed their phishing simulation outcomes and discovered that 30% of employees interacted with the dummy phishing link. The results show that employees require targeted training to better identify phishing attempts.

This section presents real-world case studies that demonstrate how organizations achieved continuous improvement in their OT cybersecurity programs.

This chapter demonstrates its concepts through real-world case studies which illustrate organizations that effectively incorporated continuous improvement and monitoring practices into their OT cybersecurity programs.

Case Study 1: A Power Generation Company

Background: The power generation company was dealing with escalating cyber threats to its SCADA systems. The cybersecurity audit revealed multiple vulnerabilities within the organization which consisted of outdated software and inadequate employee training.

Implementation of Continuous Improvement:

Regular Security Assessments: The organization conducted annual cybersecurity audits together with quarterly vulnerability assessments to maintain protection against new threats.

Employee Training Programs: The organization established a complete training curriculum to teach phishing awareness along with incident response procedures and secure OT system usage.

Monitoring and Alerts: The company implemented an SIEM solution to collect SCADA system logs while delivering real-time alerts about suspicious activities.

Results:

Within three months following their audit all identified vulnerabilities were patched by the organization.

Employees demonstrated a heightened understanding of cybersecurity threats which was reflected through better results in phishing simulations.

The monitoring system identified and counteracted a cyberattack attempt enabling the company to prevent operational disruption.

Case Study 2: A Water Treatment Facility

Background: After multiple attacks on critical infrastructure throughout the sector the water treatment facility acknowledged the need to strengthen their cybersecurity defenses. The audit identified insufficient access controls and emergency response procedures.

Implementation of Continuous Improvement:

Incident Response Plan Update: The facility revised its incident response plan to incorporate comprehensive cyber incident response procedures while ensuring all employees receive training on these updated protocols.

Implementation of Monitoring Tools: The organization installed network monitoring tools which track OT device communications and send alerts to the security team about any unusual activity.

Security Awareness Campaigns: The facility started a security awareness campaign which used posters and newsletters alongside interactive training sessions to promote cybersecurity practices among employees.

Results:

The facility prevented further damage from a cyber incident involving unauthorized access attempts by implementing their updated incident response plan which showed their preparedness had improved.

The facility employed monitoring tools which delivered actionable insights to proactively identify and address vulnerabilities.

The facility saw a substantial rise in employee engagement with security awareness initiatives, creating a stronger awareness of security throughout the organization.

Case Study 3: A Chemical Manufacturing Plant

Background: The chemical manufacturing facility was worried about how cyber threats might disrupt its production operations. The audit uncovered major deficiencies in cybersecurity methods which predominantly affected employee training and operational technology system monitoring.

Implementation of Continuous Improvement:

Comprehensive Training Program: Through its robust training program, the plant provided regular training sessions focusing on cybersecurity best practices along with incident reporting techniques and instilling a security-first mindset among employees.

Deployment of IDPS: The organization deployed an Intrusion Detection and Prevention System (IDPS) which provides real-time monitoring of network traffic to detect potential security threats.

Post-Implementation Reviews: Post-implementation reviews followed every major security initiative to evaluate effectiveness and collect feedback for future enhancements.

Results:

The training program greatly improved employee knowledge about cybersecurity threats and resulted in fewer security incidents.

The security team received alerts about multiple unauthorized access attempts from the IDPS which enabled them to take swift action and reduce potential threats.

The organization developed a continuous improvement culture by actively seeking employee feedback to enhance security practices.

Key Takeaways for Continuous Improvement and Monitoring

Adopt a Proactive Approach: To maintain a strong defense against emerging threats organizations need to focus on proactive strategies that include consistent performance assessments together with uninterrupted monitoring.

Foster a Culture of Security: When organizations involve their staff in cybersecurity measures and awareness programs they build a security-focused culture that strengthens their ability to withstand threats.

Utilize Technology Effectively: Selecting appropriate monitoring and incident response tools helps organizations maintain operational technology visibility while enabling quick threat responses.

Document and Evaluate: Organizations enhance improvement and accountability through proper documentation of their findings along with the actions undertaken and lessons identified.

Remain Agile: Organizations need to adjust their cybersecurity strategies whenever new threats emerge or regulations alter along with technological progress.

Conclusion

A strong OT cybersecurity strategy requires ongoing improvement measures alongside comprehensive monitoring protocols. Organizations must maintain continuous security posture assessments while implementing employee cybersecurity training programs and technological solutions for improved monitoring as they face changing threat landscapes.

The chapter explains why organizations must pursue ongoing enhancement and implement solid surveillance methods while building an internal culture that recognizes and values security awareness.

Phishing Simulations: Measure employee performance in recognizing and reporting phishing attempts by analyzing the outcomes of phishing simulations. The collected data enables organizations to pinpoint training deficiencies.

Example: The organization discovered through their analysis of phishing simulation results that 30% of the workforce clicked on the test phishing link. The results suggest that employees require enhanced training programs to better identify phishing attempts.

An exploration of real-world case studies demonstrates continuous improvement strategies for OT cybersecurity programs.

To demonstrate the chapter's ideas, we will review real-world organizational case studies that achieved success through continuous improvement and monitoring in their OT cybersecurity programs.

Case Study 1: A Power Generation Company

Background: A power generation company encountered rising cyber threats which aimed at its SCADA systems. The organization discovered multiple weaknesses through a cybersecurity audit which revealed that they were using outdated software, and their employees lacked adequate training.

Implementation of Continuous Improvement:

Regular Security Assessments: The company implemented annual cybersecurity audits and quarterly vulnerability assessments to maintain a proactive stance against emerging threats.

Employee Training Programs: The organization launched a detailed training curriculum covering phishing awareness along with incident response protocols and secure operational technology system usage.

Monitoring and Alerts: The organization implemented a SIEM solution to consolidate SCADA system logs and detect unusual activities through real-time alerts.

Results:

The organization fixed every vulnerability found during the audit within a three-month period.

Significant improvement in employee awareness about cybersecurity threats became evident through better results in phishing simulations.

The company's monitoring system identified and countered a cyberattack attempt which enabled them to prevent operational disruption.

Case Study 2: A Water Treatment Facility

Background: Following multiple attacks on critical infrastructure throughout the industry, a water treatment facility realized the necessity for better cybersecurity measures. The security audit exposed vulnerabilities in both access management and incident response systems.

Implementation of Continuous Improvement:

Incident Response Plan Update: The facility implemented updates to its incident response plan by adding specific procedures for handling cyber incidents and provided training for all employees on these new protocols.

Implementation of Monitoring Tools: The organization deployed network monitoring tools which track OT device communications and notify the security team when anomalies occur.

Security Awareness Campaigns: Through the launch of a security awareness campaign the facility used posters, newsletters, and interactive training sessions to involve employees in cybersecurity practices.

Results:

The facility showed improved preparedness because it successfully managed a cyber incident involving unauthorized access attempts after implementing the updated incident response plan.

The facility used monitoring tools to detect vulnerabilities early and implement preventive measures before issues developed.

The facility achieved a more security-conscious culture through significantly increased employee engagement in security awareness initiatives.

Case Study 3: A Chemical Manufacturing Plant

Background: The chemical manufacturing facility worried about how cyber threats could affect its production operations. Cybersecurity audit findings highlighted major deficiencies in staff training and operational technology system monitoring practices.

Implementation of Continuous Improvement:

Comprehensive Training Program: The plant established a strong training program which regularly covered cybersecurity best practices alongside incident reporting and fostering a security-first mentality.

Deployment of IDPS: The organization deployed an Intrusion Detection and Prevention System (IDPS) for real-time network traffic monitoring to detect potential threats as they occur.

Post-Implementation Reviews: The organization evaluated the success of major security initiatives through post-implementation reviews that collected feedback to improve future projects.

Results:

Employee awareness and understanding of cybersecurity risks soared after the comprehensive training program and this led to fewer security incidents.

Through rapid detection of several unauthorized access attempts by the IDPS the security team was able to respond swiftly to neutralize potential threats.

The organization built a continuous improvement culture by actively seeking employee feedback to enhance security practices.

Key Takeaways for Continuous Improvement and Monitoring

Adopt a Proactive Approach: To effectively manage emerging threats organizations need to implement proactive strategies that include consistent assessments and ongoing monitoring.

Foster a Culture of Security: When companies involve their employees in cybersecurity efforts and awareness programs they create a security-focused environment that strengthens their total resilience.

Utilize Technology Effectively: The selection of appropriate monitoring and incident response tools is essential to ensure visibility into the OT environment and enable swift threat responses.

Document and Evaluate: An organization can improve continuously and maintain accountability through thorough documentation of its findings and the resulting actions and lessons learned.

Remain Agile: Organizations need to modify their cybersecurity procedures to address evolving threats alongside new regulations and technological progress.

Conclusion

A strong OT cybersecurity strategy requires constant improvement and ongoing monitoring to remain effective. Organizations need to maintain regular security assessments while training staff about cybersecurity issues and implementing technological tools to improve monitoring throughout the ever-changing threat environment.

The chapter emphasizes the requirement for ongoing enhancement along with the development of efficient monitoring systems and the creation of an organizational culture that values security awareness.

Phishing Simulations: Phishing simulation results provide metrics on how well employees identify and report phishing attacks. Analyzed data reveals areas that require training improvement efforts.

Example: The organization analyzed their phishing simulation results and discovered that 30% of employees clicked the simulated phishing link. The results indicate the organization requires targeted training programs to improve its employees' ability to identify phishing attacks.

This section explores real-world case studies demonstrating how organizations continuously improved their OT cybersecurity programs through practical examples.

This chapter's concepts will become clearer through examination of real-world case studies showing how organizations effectively applied continuous improvement and monitoring practices within their OT cybersecurity frameworks.

Case Study 1: A Power Generation Company

Background: The power generation company experienced a rise in cyber threats specifically aimed at its SCADA systems. The organization discovered multiple security weaknesses through a cybersecurity audit which revealed outdated software and inadequate training of employees.

Implementation of Continuous Improvement:

Regular Security Assessments: The company established annual cybersecurity audits together with quarterly vulnerability assessments to maintain their defense against emerging threats.

Employee Training Programs: Through their comprehensive training program employees learned about phishing awareness techniques alongside incident response procedures and safe operational technology system usage.

Monitoring and Alerts: The organization implemented a SIEM solution which collects SCADA system logs and generates immediate alerts for unusual activities.

Results:

All vulnerabilities identified during the audit were patched by the organization within a three-month timeframe.

Employees displayed better performance in phishing simulations which demonstrated their increased knowledge about cybersecurity threats.

When the monitoring system identified an attempted cyberattack, it initiated a response that enabled the company to neutralize the threat before operational impact occurred.

Case Study 2: A Water Treatment Facility

Background: The water treatment facility identified a need for stronger cybersecurity measures after experiencing multiple attacks against critical infrastructure facilities in the industry. The audit identified vulnerabilities within access control measures and incident response systems.

Implementation of Continuous Improvement:

Incident Response Plan Update: The facility revised its incident response plan with procedures to handle cyber incidents and conducted training sessions for employees to familiarize them with the updated protocols.

Implementation of Monitoring Tools: The organization deployed network monitoring tools that enabled tracking of communication between OT devices and provided alerts to the security team when anomalies occurred.

Security Awareness Campaigns: The facility introduced a cybersecurity awareness program which involved posters and newsletters and interactive training sessions to engage employees with cybersecurity practices.

Results:

The facility demonstrated improved preparedness by successfully containing a cyber incident involving unauthorized access attempts after applying the updated incident response plan.

The facility used monitoring tools to gain actionable insights which enabled proactive identification and mitigation of vulnerabilities.

The facility achieved a stronger security-conscious culture because employee participation in security awareness initiatives rose significantly.

Case Study 3: A Chemical Manufacturing Plant

Background: The chemical manufacturing plant expressed worry about how cyber threats could impact its production activities. A cybersecurity audit identified major deficiencies related to staff training programs and operational technology system monitoring.

Implementation of Continuous Improvement:

Comprehensive Training Program: The plant created a strong training program which held regular sessions about cybersecurity, the best practices along with incident reporting and teaching employees to maintain a security-first mindset.

Deployment of IDPS: The organization activated an Intrusion Detection and Prevention System (IDPS) which allows real-time monitoring of network traffic to detect potential threats.

Post-Implementation Reviews: The organization conducted post-implementation reviews to evaluate effectiveness and collect feedback after completing every major security initiative.

Results:

The organization's complete training program enhanced employee understanding of cybersecurity threats which resulted in fewer security incidents.

The security team benefited from the IDPS's ability to detect multiple unauthorized access attempts enabling them to respond promptly to potential threats.

The organization cultivated a continuous improvement atmosphere by actively gathering employee feedback to enhance security practices.

Key Takeaways for Continuous Improvement and Monitoring

Adopt a Proactive Approach: To remain ahead of evolving threats organizations should make regular assessments and continuous monitoring their top security priorities.

Foster a Culture of Security: When companies actively involve their staff in cybersecurity efforts and promote awareness, they build a protective culture that strengthens their defenses.

Utilize Technology Effectively: The implementation of appropriate monitoring and incident response tools is essential to maintain visibility of the OT environment and enable quick threat response.

Document and Evaluate: Proper documentation of results and corrective measures along with learned lessons drives organizational growth and responsibility.

Remain Agile: Businesses must adjust their cybersecurity procedures to tackle evolving threats alongside new regulations and technological progress.

Conclusion

A strong OT cybersecurity approach requires ongoing enhancement and consistent monitoring. Organizations must assess their security posture regularly while both enhancing employees' cybersecurity awareness and leveraging technology to improve monitoring capabilities as they face changing threats.

The chapter demonstrates why organizations need to constantly improve their security measures while developing effective monitoring systems and promoting a security-aware culture. The analysis of real-world case studies demonstrated how organizations can effectively apply these principles to bolster their cybersecurity defenses.

Organizations that implement continuous improvement and strong monitoring practices will achieve better protection of their essential infrastructure and operational stability while facing rising cyber threats in OT environments. The upcoming chapters will showcase further tools and methods to advance OT cybersecurity capabilities while offering readers practical guidance to implement in their own operational settings.

Implementing Continuous Improvement: A Step-by-Step Guide

Organizations need to follow a systematic approach combining assessment activities with action steps and evaluation procedures for successful continuous improvement in OT cybersecurity. This manual describes the essential procedures to establish a culture focused on continuous improvement and active monitoring.

Step 1: Conduct Regular Security Assessments

Overview: Organizations benefit from regular security assessments because they reveal vulnerabilities and allow evaluation of control effectiveness while ensuring regulatory compliance.

Actions:

Establish a Schedule: Implement a consistent schedule for security evaluations that involves penetration testing along with vulnerability assessments and compliance audits. The timing of security assessments should align with organizational requirements and could occur quarterly, bi-annually or annually.

Example: The pharmaceutical company ensures its OT systems stay secure and compliant by implementing vulnerability assessments twice per year and compliance audits every year.

Use Diverse Assessment Methods: A comprehensive understanding of security posture requires both automated tools and manual assessment methods.

Example: Security professionals utilize automated vulnerability scanning software such as Nessus together with manual penetration testing methods to detect both well-known weaknesses and possible threats that automated systems might overlook.

Step 2: Analyze Assessment Results

Overview: Organizations need to evaluate assessment outcomes to discover patterns and improvement opportunities while detecting new security risks.

Actions:

Aggregate Findings: Create a unified report that summarizes findings from multiple assessments and focuses on vulnerabilities alongside compliance issues and identified concerns.

Example: Following security assessments, the audit team prepares a report that documents the discovered vulnerabilities along with their severity levels as well as the status of remediation efforts.

Identify Patterns and Trends: Monitor vulnerability patterns over time to detect recurring problems and areas that frequently become weak points. Organizations should utilize this analysis to improve upcoming training programs and security strategies.

Example: A security team discovers numerous vulnerabilities stem from outdated software and initiates a program to improve patch management practices and personnel training about system updates.

Step 3: Develop and Update Action Plans

Overview: Organizations must develop new action plans or revise existing ones to address discovered vulnerabilities and improve their cybersecurity defenses based on assessment findings.

Actions:

Prioritize Action Items: Organizations should prioritize action items for remediation according to the severity levels and operational impact found in risk assessment reports.

Example: The action plan addresses critical SCADA system vulnerabilities as top priority while planning remediation for medium-priority items at later stages.

Incorporate Lessons Learned: Use historical incident data and audit results to develop an action plan that prevents the recurrence of former errors.

Example: The organization will immediately enforce stronger access controls alongside conducting employee training on password management following a data breach caused by inadequate access controls.

Step 4: Implement Remediation Measures

Overview: The organization should enhance its cybersecurity posture by putting the required remediation measures into action as specified by the action plan.

Actions:

Assign Responsibilities: Assign clear responsibilities to people or teams for every action item in the plan to create a sense of accountability.

Example: The IT team handles software updates, and the OT team manages changes to access control measures.

Monitor Progress: Project management tools help monitor action item status while ensuring they complete on schedule.

Example: The project management dashboard displays the progress of each action item so stakeholders can quickly assess status updates.

Step 5: Continuous Monitoring and Evaluation

Overview: Set up a continuous monitoring program to track security events and evaluate the performance of security measures.

Actions:

Deploy Monitoring Tools: Implement monitoring tools to identify anomalies and track compliance while generating real-time alerts for potential incidents.

Example: The organization's SIEM system monitors logs from IT and OT environments to provide centralized visibility and alerts for suspicious activities.

Regularly Review Monitoring Data: Perform consistent evaluations of monitoring data to discover patterns and determine security measure performance while improving monitoring approaches.

Example: The security team meets every week to analyze monitoring alerts and incident discussions while documenting and sharing organizational lessons learned.

Step 6: Foster Culture of Security Awareness

Overview: The development of a security awareness culture remains essential to make sure every employee knows their function in cybersecurity protection.

Actions:

Engage Employees in Security Programs: Employees should become part of security projects and be motivated to join training programs.

Example: During "Cybersecurity Awareness Week" the organization arranges workshops and guest speaker sessions along with interactive activities to teach employees about methods for protecting against cybersecurity threats. The organization invites employees to communicate their security difficulties and participate in role-specific security discussions.

Recognize and Reward Vigilance: Establish reward systems for staff members who show strong security behavior or identify potential threats.

Example: The organization rewards employees who report phishing attempts or suspicious activities with gifts cards and public recognition through company communications.

Step 7: Evaluate and Adjust

Overview: Organizations must regularly assess their cybersecurity strategies to identify their effectiveness and make necessary adjustments to ensure continuous improvement.

Actions:

Conduct Post-Implementation Reviews: Perform assessments and collect feedback from teams following major remediation activities to evaluate their success.

Example: The organization holds a review meeting after implementing the new access controls to assess their adoption success and risk mitigation effectiveness.

Adapt to Changing Threats: Keep up to date with new security threats and make necessary adjustments to protect your organization. Revisiting the risk assessment and adjusting the action plan may become necessary.

Example: The cybersecurity team stays updated with industry news and threat intelligence reports to discover new vulnerabilities from emerging technologies and cyber-attack patterns for proactive organizational defense.

Conclusion

A strong OT cybersecurity strategy requires ongoing monitoring combined with continuous improvement efforts. Organizations can protect themselves against changing cyber threats by implementing a structured strategy composed of regular assessments along with ongoing training and effective monitoring processes.

This chapter explained how organizations can achieve continuous OT cybersecurity enhancement through consistent security evaluations and feedback systems along with regular training sessions and promoting a security-focused company culture. Organizations which adopt these strategic practices will maintain enhanced protection over their essential infrastructure while sustaining operational resilience amid constantly evolving cyber threats.

The upcoming chapters discuss both technological solutions and successful organizational practices for OT cybersecurity through continuous monitoring and improvement methods. The insights offered here serve as practical advice for organizations aiming to improve their cybersecurity measures within operational technology's complex environment.

This marks the ending of Chapter 9 in "The OT Cybersecurity Audit Handbook: Strategies for Success." The upcoming chapters will explore various tools and technologies alongside specific methodologies which organizations can use to enhance their continuous improvement and monitoring processes and examine case studies demonstrating effective OT environment implementations. The insights presented will enable organizations to manage OT cybersecurity challenges successfully and improve their security posture.

Chapter 10: Tools and Technologies for Enhancing OT Cybersecurity

Introduction

Operational Technology (OT) cybersecurity presents multiple challenges across its complex landscape which demand specific tailored solutions. The adoption of advanced technologies and interconnected systems by organizations makes it essential to utilize effective tools and technologies. This chapter examines multiple tools and technologies available to strengthen OT cybersecurity through vulnerability management protocols as well as monitoring systems and incident response capabilities together with threat intelligence solutions. This section delivers examples of top solutions for each category and explores organizational methods for incorporating these tools into security strategies.

1. Vulnerability Management Tools

Vulnerability management stands as an essential element of OT cybersecurity because it allows organizations to discover vulnerabilities and act through assessment and remediation of system and application weaknesses. Through efficient vulnerability management utilities organizations can speed up their security processes while maintaining a strong defense against threats.

1.1. Vulnerability Scanners

Overview: Vulnerability scanners function as automated tools which evaluate systems to detect known vulnerabilities as well as misconfigurations and compliance issues. These scanners give organizations visibility into their security deficits which enables them to execute timely fixes.

Key Features:

Automated Scanning: Automated tools assess networks, systems, and applications by matching them against known vulnerabilities from databases such as the National Vulnerability Database (NVD).

Reporting: Create comprehensive reports which detail vulnerabilities that have been detected along with their criticality levels and suggested corrective actions.

Examples:

Nessus: Nessus stands as a leading vulnerability scanner because it provides extensive scanning functions for both IT and OT environments. This system identifies software vulnerabilities, configuration errors and compliance problems.

Use Case: The manufacturing plant scans its SCADA systems with Nessus which reveals multiple versions of outdated software. The team focuses on addressing vulnerabilities through patches to stop possible exploitation.

Qualys: This cloud-based vulnerability management solution delivers ongoing monitoring and vulnerability scanning which helps organizations keep their security posture current.

Use Case: Through Qualys, the energy company maintains continuous surveillance of its OT environment to obtain immediate alerts about any new vulnerabilities that could affect essential infrastructure.

1.2. Configuration Management Tools

Overview: Configuration management tools enable organizations to evaluate system and device configurations according to established security benchmarks. The tools verify that OT system configurations meet security standards while following best practice guidelines.

Key Features:

Baseline Configuration Assessment: Analyze present system settings against established security standards to detect any differences.

Change Tracking: Use configuration management tools to track configuration changes and notify administrators when unauthorized modifications occur.

Examples:

CIS-CAT: The Center for Internet Security Configuration Assessment Tool (CIS-CAT) analyzes system configurations based on CIS benchmarks to deliver practical security hardening recommendations.

Use Case: The water treatment facility utilizes CIS-CAT to examine PLC configurations to verify security standard compliance.

Tripwire: This tool tracks system configurations and file integrity to alert users about unauthorized changes which may signal security issues.

Use Case: The chemical manufacturing plant utilizes Tripwire to supervise OT systems and identify unauthorized modifications to configuration files that threaten security.

2. Monitoring Tools

OT environments require continuous monitoring to identify anomalies and threats. These tools enable organizations to achieve system visibility while allowing them to respond effectively to security incidents.

2.1. Security Information and Event Management (SIEM) Solutions

Overview: SIEM solutions collect security data from various sources to analyze them and provide real-time monitoring insights along with alerts for potential security incidents.

Key Features:

Log Management: Analyze logs coming from OT systems, networks, and applications to detect abnormal patterns.

Real-Time Alerts: Create alerts through specific rules and limits to enable rapid incident response.

Examples:

Splunk: Splunk serves as a robust SIEM platform which allows configuration for OT system monitoring and log collection from multiple sources to enable full-scale analysis and alerting.

Use Case: Splunk helps an energy utility monitor its OT environment to detect anomalies. The SIEM system notifies security personnel about suspicious login attempts to essential systems to facilitate prompt investigation.

IBM QRadar: The SIEM solution combines sophisticated analytics with machine learning technology to find unusual patterns in OT systems.

Use Case: The pharmaceutical company uses QRadar to monitor security events throughout its manufacturing systems which improves its threat detection and response capabilities.

2.2. Network Monitoring Tools

Overview: Network monitoring tools examine real-time network traffic to detect anomalies and threats that affect OT environments.

Key Features:

Traffic Analysis: Examine network traffic patterns to identify abnormal activities that might reveal cyber threats.

Protocol Analysis: Review of OT system communication protocols to confirm they meet expected standards.

Examples:

SolarWinds Network Performance Monitor: This tool enables organizations to maintain network performance and security visibility while identifying anomalous OT communication patterns.

Use Case: SolarWinds serves as the network monitoring solution for a chemical processing facility. Unusual transmission spikes between devices detected by the tool lead security teams to probe possible unauthorized communications.

Darktrace: The platform uses AI-driven machine learning algorithms to detect threats as they happen by analyzing normal behavioral patterns.

Use Case: Darktrace provides monitoring services for an energy company's OT network traffic. The AI system detects unusual data flows from operational devices to external IP addresses that prompt immediate alert notifications for investigation.

2.3. Intrusion Detection and Prevention Systems (IDPS)

Overview: IDPS technology monitors network and system operations to detect harmful activities and breaches while issuing alerts and executing actions according to established protocols.

Key Features:

Signature-Based Detection: Identify known threats based on predefined signatures.

Anomaly-Based Detection: Spot abnormal behavior patterns that might signal the presence of previously unidentified threats.

Examples:

Snort: Snort serves as an open-source intrusion detection system that enables users to track network traffic and identify suspicious activities relevant to operational technology environments.

Use Case: The manufacturing facility runs Snort as its primary tool for monitoring SCADA network communications to detect intrusion attempts and generate alerts for the security team to investigate.

Cisco Firepower: Cisco Firepower delivers a complete security solution designed with intrusion prevention features to protect industrial settings.

Use Case: A water utility deploys Cisco Firepower to actively track network threats which permits real-time blocking of unauthorized access attempts.

3. Incident Response Tools

Organizations require incident response tools to handle cybersecurity incidents since they help detect threats and enable efficient responses and recovery processes.

3.1. Incident Response Platforms

Overview: Cybersecurity incident management platforms deliver functional workflows and automated processes along with documentation features.

Key Features:

Incident Tracking: Create a centralized system that tracks incidents through their entire lifecycle from detection to resolution.

Playbooks and Automation: Support incident response efforts by supplying pre-set playbooks together with automation tools to increase response efficiency.

Examples:

Splunk Phantom: This security orchestration and automation platform enables organizations to automate their incident response procedures while enhancing response time efficiency.

Use Case: A pharmaceutical company implemented Splunk Phantom to automate its incident response operations and enable its security team to quickly address alerts while minimizing human mistakes during incidents.

IBM Resilient: IBM Resilient gives incident responders' documentation tools and collaboration options while enabling workflow management during all stages of incident management.

Use Case: The utility company uses IBM Resilient to manage its cybersecurity incident responses while keeping team members updated and ensuring tasks are completed efficiently.

3.2. Forensic Analysis Tools

Overview: Security professionals use forensic analysis tools to investigate security incidents and determine both the method of attack and its consequences.

Key Features:

Data Recovery: Analyze data together with recovered deleted files to discover the attack methodology.

Timeline Creation: Develop event timelines to decipher the sequence of actions executed during a security incident.

Examples:

EnCase: The EnCase tool enables organizations to conduct thorough investigations and collect cyber incident evidence through its forensic analysis capabilities.

Use Case: The security team utilizes EnCase to inspect compromised systems and determine the methods attackers employed to gain access following a data breach.

FTK (Forensic Toolkit): This forensic analysis tool facilitates digital evidence collection and analysis from multiple sources for investigative reporting.

Use Case: The manufacturing organization uses FTK for a forensic investigation following suspicious network activity detection which helps them determine how far the breach has spread.

4. Threat Intelligence Tools

Organizations use threat intelligence tools to gain understanding of new threats and vulnerabilities along with attacker methods which support proactive cybersecurity defense strategies.

4.1. Threat Intelligence Platforms (TIP)

Overview: Threat intelligence platforms gather information from numerous sources for organizations to analyze data correlations and detect threats.

Key Features:

Data Aggregation: Gather threat intelligence data from open-source feeds, commercial vendors, and internal sources.

Correlation and Analysis: Examine threat data and establish relationships between different pieces of information to detect patterns and future risks.

Examples:

Recorded Future: The threat intelligence platform delivers real-time threat and vulnerability insights for organizations to establish effective cybersecurity strategies.

Use Case: The energy company employs Recorded Future to monitor new threats within its sector which enables proactive security adjustments.

ThreatConnect: ThreatConnect provides organizations with a platform to collect threat intelligence data which can be analyzed and used to inform security actions.

ThreatConnect empowers organizations to incorporate threat intelligence data into their security operations. The organization improves its threat detection and response capabilities by linking threat data with its current security tools to achieve real-time operations.

4.2. Open-Source Threat Intelligence

Overview: Open-source threat intelligence offers organizations access to public data about security threats and vulnerabilities and attack methods. Organizations can strengthen their security measures through public threat data without facing substantial expenses.

Key Features:

Community Contributions: Security experts alongside researchers and organizations generate open-source intelligence which provides a variety of analytical perspectives.

Regular Updates: Organizations receive up-to-date information about new threats through sources that receive regular updates.

Examples:

AlienVault Open Threat Exchange (OTX): The platform enables security experts to exchange threat intelligence and strategic insights through collaborative interactions.

Use Case: The manufacturing facility utilizes OTX to receive updates about new malware strains and attack vectors in similar sectors which enables them to update their defenses as needed.

Virus Total: This service examines suspicious files and URLs for malware detection and distributes results automatically to the community.

Use Case: The energy company analyzes employee-submitted files with Virus Total to detect malware and block infected files from accessing the network.

5. Integrating Tools into an OT Cybersecurity Strategy

Organizations need to build a unified cybersecurity strategy that merges different tools and technologies based on their specific operational requirements and needs to effectively improve OT cybersecurity.

5.1. Developing a Comprehensive Cybersecurity Framework

Overview: A complete cybersecurity framework delivers an organized method for addressing cybersecurity threats and unifying different tools and technologies.

Actions:

Adopt Established Frameworks: The organization's cybersecurity strategy development should utilize established cybersecurity frameworks like the NIST Cybersecurity Framework or the ISO/IEC 27001 standard.

Example: To structure its cybersecurity initiatives the utility company adopts the NIST Cybersecurity Framework which ensures that its tools and technologies follow best practices for risk management.

Define Security Objectives: Develop security goals that support both business targets and necessary legal standards. The organization's cybersecurity work consistently reinforces its principal mission.

Example: The organization establishes security objectives that focus on safeguarding critical infrastructure while meeting regulatory standards and reducing operational interruptions.

5.2. Ensuring Interoperability

Overview: Organizations need to guarantee compatibility between different security solutions to achieve maximum effectiveness from their security tools. Data sharing becomes more efficient while overall security improvements occur through this process.

Actions:

Select Compatible Tools: Organizations should select security tools that provide seamless integration with their current systems while enabling efficient data sharing. The selection process should include tools which have support for shared protocols and APIs.

Example: The organization picks a SIEM system that could ingest logs from multiple monitoring tools which allow centralized visibility and analysis of security events.

Establish Data Sharing Protocols: Develop data sharing protocols among security tools to create a unified strategy for detecting and responding to threats.

Example: By setting up data-sharing protocols between its vulnerability scanner and SIEM system a chemical plant enables automatic alerts to be generated in the SIEM whenever vulnerabilities are discovered to facilitate further examination.

5.3. Continuous Evaluation and Adaptation

Overview: Organizations need to constantly assess and update their security strategies and technologies due to the ever-evolving cybersecurity environment.

Actions:

Regularly Review Tool Effectiveness: Conduct regular evaluations to ensure the tools and technologies currently in use are performing effectively. Organizations need to assess tool performance and identify gaps before implementing required adjustments.

Example: The manufacturing organization conducts yearly evaluations of its monitoring tools to determine their effectiveness in threat detection and response. After reviewing their current systems, the organization selects an updated network monitoring solution for better threat detection capabilities.

Stay Informed About Emerging Technologies: Stay updated on new developments and current trends within the cybersecurity sector. Assess the potential impact of new tools on strengthening current security operations.

Example: The cybersecurity team reads industry publications and attends conferences to discover innovative technologies that could enhance their security posture including AI-driven threat detection tools.

Conclusion

Organizations need to deploy multiple tools and technologies to strengthen their OT cybersecurity defenses against evolving cyber threats. Organizations that deploy effective vulnerability management and monitoring systems alongside incident response and threat intelligence tools significantly boost their security posture.

This chapter reviewed several types of cybersecurity tools for OT environments including vulnerability management systems, monitoring solutions as well as incident response platforms and threat intelligence resources. The discussion highlighted the need for organizations to embed these tools into their cybersecurity strategy to maintain constant improvement and adaptability.

Organizations that enhance their cybersecurity defenses will secure their essential infrastructure better while maintaining their operational processes. The next chapters will explore detailed case studies of organizations that implemented these tools and technologies to gain actionable insights for readers aiming to improve their cybersecurity methods in operational technology settings.

We have reached the end of Chapter 10 in "The OT Cybersecurity Audit Handbook: Strategies for Success." The subsequent chapters will analyze case studies demonstrating organizational success in implementing these tools and technologies in their operational technology settings. Our organization offers actionable insights and best practices that organizations can use to handle OT cybersecurity challenges and strengthen their security measures.

Organizations need to understand OT cybersecurity tool implementation through practical case studies.

We will analyze multiple case studies of companies that have successfully deployed these discussed tools and technologies to demonstrate effective cybersecurity implementation.

Case Study 1: A Power Generation Company

Background: The power generation company maintains essential assets such as turbines and grid management systems which play a vital role in supplying national energy. After enduring multiple cyberattacks against critical infrastructure elements the company moved to upgrade its cybersecurity defenses.

Implementation of Tools:

Vulnerability Management: The organization implemented Qualys to automate vulnerability scans throughout its OT infrastructure. The tool detected both outdated software versions and incorrect configurations within the company's SCADA systems.

Outcome: After three months of deployment the company resolved 95% of discovered vulnerabilities which led to a major reduction in its attack surface.

Monitoring Solutions: The organization chose Splunk as its SIEM system to collect logs from network devices and SCADA systems along with other sources. Centralized visibility allowed the system to detect anomalies in real-time.

Outcome: Splunk enabled the security team to respond promptly by generating actionable alerts when suspicious activities occurred. The SIEM solution alerted the team about unauthorized login attempts from an external IP address enabling swift mitigation action.

Incident Response: The adoption of IBM Resilient enabled the company to optimize incident response operations which improved their security team's coordination and workflow management.

Outcome: The response team used IBM Resilient to record details of the minor unauthorized access attempt incident and then analyzed their response while updating their incident response plan with insights gained.

Case Study 2: A Water Treatment Facility

Background: The municipal water treatment facility encountered stricter regulatory evaluations and reputational risks because of cybersecurity threats. The facility acknowledged the necessity for improved security protections to safeguard its OT systems.

Implementation of Tools:

Network Monitoring: The facility deployed Darktrace technology to maintain continuous oversight of network traffic. Darktrace's AI technology learned standard network traffic patterns which allowed it to detect deviations that suggested potential security risks.

Outcome: Darktrace discovered an abnormal data exfiltration pattern from a PLC which led to an investigation that revealed an insider threat. Security measures allowed resolution of the situation before any sensitive information became compromised.

Threat Intelligence: The organization signed up for Recorded Future services to obtain specialized threat information for the water sector. By adopting this proactive strategy, the organization maintained superior control over emerging risks.

Outcome: The facility used threat intelligence to establish preventive actions against a newly discovered vulnerability threatening water treatment systems within industry.

Training and Awareness: Staff training programs at the facility became comprehensive through input from the security team and incident analysis.

Outcome: Regular training sessions led to marked enhancements in employee cybersecurity knowledge which resulted in a 60% reduction in phishing incidents reported.

Case Study 3: A Manufacturing Plant

Background: The large manufacturing plant became aware of potential risks to its interconnected OT systems once it learned about cyberattacks that targeted similar facilities. The company worked to strengthen its cybersecurity defenses by implementing a full suite of tools.

Implementation of Tools:

Vulnerability Scanning: Nessus received deployment at the manufacturing plant to carry out routine vulnerability assessments of its OT systems. The vulnerability tool successfully detected multiple security weaknesses in both PLCs and HMIs.

Outcome: The plant achieved an 80% reduction in its overall vulnerability count in six months through prioritized remediation based on Nessus findings.

Incident Response Platform: Through the integration of Splunk Phantom the organization automated its incident response capabilities, which enabled the security team to handle alerts more effectively.

Outcome: Response workflow automation led to a 40% reduction in the average response time to security incidents which improved the plant's threat management capabilities.

Security Awareness Campaign: The plant launched a security awareness campaign which focused on the significance of cybersecurity for operational safety. The program used interactive training sessions along with gamification methods to keep employees actively involved.

Outcome: The campaign resulted in both higher employee involvement in security initiatives and stronger personal accountability for security practices.

Best Practices for Tool Implementation

Organizations which analyze case studies about effective tools and technology implementations should adopt the best practices to achieve successful deployment and integration.

1. Conduct a Needs Assessment

Overview: Organizations need to perform an in-depth evaluation of their specific requirements, accounting for existing vulnerabilities along with regulatory demands and operational limitations before they choose their tools.

Actions:

Identify Gaps in Current Security: Evaluate current security protocols through a detailed examination to uncover deficiencies and potential improvement opportunities. Organizations need to perform vulnerability assessments and employee interviews as well as audit existing policies and procedures to identify gaps.

Example: Gap analysis at a manufacturing plant detects outdated incident response procedures and insufficient integration of monitoring tools with other security solutions. The assessment process guides decision-makers in choosing new tools and technologies.

Assess Regulatory Compliance: Industry-specific regulatory requirements must be part of the evaluation process for potential tools. The organization can avoid legal consequences and improve its reputation through proper compliance measures.

Example: The utility company emphasizes NERC CIP compliance as an essential aspect of its tool selection procedure and gives priority to systems that deliver strong reporting functions to fulfill regulatory requirements.

2. Choose Scalable Solutions

Overview: Growing organizations must choose tools that possess the ability to scale in line with their expanding operational requirements.

Actions:

Evaluate Scalability: Verify if the tools have the capacity to handle future increases in data volumes and user numbers along with expanded functionalities.

Example: The water treatment facility chooses a SIEM solution that allows effortless integration with new data sources as OT devices join the network to maintain complete security monitoring.

Consider Future Growth: Select solutions capable of evolving alongside both technological improvements and threat landscape shifts to maintain lasting effectiveness.

Example: The pharmaceutical company commits resources to a cybersecurity framework featuring advanced analytics and machine learning to prepare for upcoming threats and improve detection effectiveness.

3. Plan for Integration

Overview: The seamless merging of new security tools into existing systems proves essential to achieve maximum protection while reducing operational interruptions.

Actions:

Assess Compatibility: Evaluate the integration capabilities of new tools with current security solutions and operational technologies before implementation.

Example: The chemical plant conducts an evaluation of the new vulnerability scanner's compatibility with its current SIEM system to establish uninterrupted data transmission and analysis capabilities.

Develop an Integration Strategy: Develop a comprehensive integration plan detailing implementation step for new tools along with timelines for execution and resource allocation alongside testing procedures.

Example: The organization implements a phased integration strategy for their new monitoring tool by first launching a pilot program in a limited environment and then proceeding to full deployment across all OT systems.

4. Provide Comprehensive Training

Overview: Organizations must train their employees in new tools and technologies to ensure these systems are used effectively and to maximize investment returns.

Actions:

Conduct Initial Training: Organize introductory training sessions where employees learn to use the new tools through practical exercises and demonstrations.

Example: The energy company delivers multiple training workshops to its IT and OT teams which cover the features and functionalities of their new SIEM solution and ensure all users become proficient with the system.

Establish Ongoing Training: Employees need to stay informed about new features and best practices as well as emerging threats through ongoing training programs.

Example: Every quarter a manufacturing plant runs refresher training sessions for employees to examine their cybersecurity tools and explore recent security incidents and vulnerabilities.

5. Monitor Effectiveness

Overview: Organizations need to conduct ongoing evaluations of new tools to verify that they fulfill security goals.

Actions:

Establish KPIs: Establish performance metrics to assess how well implemented tools address security risks and enhance cybersecurity posture.

Example: The water treatment facility defines KPIs for their new monitoring tool which measures detected anomalies count, response times to alerts and the rate of false positives detected.

Conduct Regular Reviews: Implement regular assessments of tool performance against KPIs while collecting user feedback on their experiences.

Example: The cybersecurity team at the manufacturing plant performs bi-annual evaluations of their incident response platform to analyze its performance in handling security incidents and implements team feedback to make required adjustments.

Conclusion

Successful deployment of cybersecurity tools and technologies constitutes a foundational element for strengthening OT cybersecurity defenses. Organizations can build stronger cyber defenses through a strategic selection of solutions that meet their specific needs along with developing security awareness among employees and maintaining dedication to ongoing improvements.

This chapter explored multiple types of tools that improve OT cybersecurity through vulnerability management, monitoring, incident response, and threat intelligence solutions. Our discussion included best practices for tool implementation while ensuring interoperability and ongoing assessment of effectiveness.

Organizations can safeguard their critical infrastructure and preserve operational continuity by utilizing appropriate tools and technologies to tackle the complexity of modern cybersecurity threats. The upcoming chapters present detailed case studies about organizations that have achieved success through these tools and technologies to give readers practical insights they can use in their settings.

The final section of Chapter 10 in "The OT Cybersecurity Audit Handbook: Strategies for Success" concludes here. The upcoming chapters will present detailed case studies and practical examples from organizations which have overcome OT cybersecurity audit challenges successfully.

Chapter 11: Case Studies in OT Cybersecurity Audits

Introduction

Organizations aiming to strengthen their cyber defenses need to understand how cybersecurity audits impact Operational Technology (OT) settings. This chapter showcases numerous case studies which demonstrate how multiple organizations from different industries conducted effective OT cybersecurity audits and strengthened their security frameworks by addressing vulnerabilities. The case studies presented will demonstrate both the distinct challenges encountered and the audit methodologies used along with findings and subsequent actions to strengthen cybersecurity defenses. Our collection of real-world examples offers organizations detailed insights and tested strategies to strengthen their cybersecurity operations.

Case Study 1: A Power Generation Company

Background

The power generation company maintains multiple vital assets that deliver essential electricity services. In response to the growing threat environment, the company chose to perform an extensive OT cybersecurity examination. The company's objective was to identify weaknesses within its Supervisory Control and Data Acquisition (SCADA) systems while confirming adherence to standards like NERC CIP.

Audit Methodology

The company implemented a risk-based audit approach to focus its resources on the most critical systems while evaluating vulnerabilities that could pose risks.

Risk Assessment: Through their comprehensive risk assessment process the audit team pinpointed essential assets along with potential dangers and system weaknesses. The audit team sorted risks into three levels named high, medium and low according to their potential effects on operations and safety.

Interviews and Document Review: Through interviews with essential personnel from IT and OT departments the team gathered information about current security practices. The audit team examined current documentation such as incident response plans and security policies.

Findings

The audit revealed several key findings:

Outdated Software: Outdated software versions on numerous PLCs and SCADA components left the systems vulnerable to known security threats.

Weak Access Controls: The existing access controls failed to protect critical systems from unauthorized personnel access.

Lack of Security Awareness Training: The audit found that most employees lacked sufficient knowledge of cybersecurity measures and how to respond to incidents.

Action Taken

The audit findings led the company to execute specific corrective actions.

Patching and Updates: The IT team worked on updating outdated software on critical systems as their main priority. The company set up a timetable for periodic updates in the future.

Enhanced Access Controls: The business established role-based access controls (RBAC) to ensure system access for critical systems matched job responsibilities. The company implemented multi-factor authentication (MFA) across all remote access points.

Security Awareness Training: We developed a complete training program and delivered it to all employees so they could learn cybersecurity best practices along with incident response procedures and how to report suspicious activities.

Results

The power generation company observed substantial enhancements in its cybersecurity posture after putting the new measures into action.

Reduction in Vulnerabilities: By addressing 95% of identified vulnerabilities the company managed to reduce its risk exposure within a three-month timeframe.

Improved Incident Response: Employees who received enhanced training showed improved threat awareness and faster reporting of suspicious activities which led to quicker incident detection and response.

Regulatory Compliance: After meeting NERC CIP standards, the company gained better relationships with regulatory bodies.

Case Study 2: A Water Treatment Facility

Background

The municipal water treatment facility developed concerns about its cybersecurity defenses after witnessing multiple severe cyber incidents within the water sector. The facility decided to conduct an OT cybersecurity audit to identify vulnerabilities and improve its security protocols.

Audit Methodology

The facility used a compliance-based audit approach to verify its adherence to industry regulations and standards.

Regulatory Review: The audit team first identified every applicable regulation and standard for the water sector including both EPA guidelines and state-specific rules.

Comprehensive Document Review: The team conducted an analysis of current security policies and incident response plans along with previous audit reports to find compliance deficiencies.

Technical Assessments: The facility's SCADA systems underwent vulnerability scans and penetration testing to discover potential security weaknesses.

Findings

The audit uncovered several critical findings:

Inadequate Incident Response Plan: The current incident response plan no longer meets regulatory requirements because it is outdated.

Insufficient Monitoring: The facility did not have sufficient monitoring tools to identify anomalies in network traffic and system behavior.

Unsecured Remote Access: The security measures for remote access to OT systems were inadequate which led to increased vulnerability to unauthorized access.

Action Taken

The water treatment facility implemented several corrective actions because of the audit findings.

Incident Response Plan Update: The facility updated its incident response plan to meet regulatory standards while incorporating specific protocols to handle different incident situations.

Deployment of Monitoring Tools: The water treatment facility purchased network monitoring tools which enabled real-time network traffic visibility. The security team received notifications about suspicious activities through the configuration of these tools.

Secure Remote Access: To prevent unauthorized access to OT systems the facility deployed secure remote access protocols which use VPNs and MFA.

Results

The water treatment facility achieved substantial enhancements in cybersecurity defenses after these protective strategies were put into place.

Enhanced Incident Response: The facility achieved better incident management capabilities with its updated response plan. The facility demonstrated enhanced team coordination and readiness when they followed the updated protocol during a simulated attack.

Real-Time Threat Detection: Real-time detection and response to network traffic anomalies became possible after the installation of monitoring tools. The monitoring system detected unusual data flows and enabled the team to identify and eliminate a possible malware threat before it affected operations.

Increased Confidence in Security Measures: The training and updates implemented by the organization led employees to develop greater confidence in their security measures. The organizational culture change drove a proactive cybersecurity approach as employees took active roles in detecting and alerting security threats.

Case Study 3: A Chemical Manufacturing Plant

Background

The major chemical manufacturing company received growing attention for its cybersecurity measures because its operations involved sensitive activities. The organization decided to strengthen its security protections after evaluating its OT systems through a cybersecurity audit.

Audit Methodology

The organization established an audit approach that combines both risk assessment and compliance evaluation into one integrated methodology.

Risk Assessment: The audit team performed an extensive risk assessment to pinpoint essential assets and potential threats and vulnerabilities within the chemical manufacturing process.

Compliance Evaluation: The audit team conducted a compliance check against applicable industry standards such as ISO/IEC 27001 and chemical industry regulations.

Technical Assessments: Through vulnerability scans and penetration tests the audit team pinpointed technical vulnerabilities within the OT environment.

Findings

The audit identified multiple vital vulnerabilities and compliance issues.

Inconsistent Security Policies: Different departments within the organization operated without standardized security policies which resulted in inconsistent security practices and multiple security gaps.

Weaknesses in Physical Security: Physical security measures at the facility did not meet necessary standards resulting in unauthorized personnel gaining access to important areas.

Outdated Training Programs: Cybersecurity training sessions for employees occurred too rarely to address modern threats and best security practices.

Action Taken

The chemical manufacturing plant executed multiple essential actions following insights from its audit report.

Standardization of Security Policies: By developing standardized security policies for all departments the organization achieved uniform security practices throughout the organization.

Enhancement of Physical Security: The facility strengthened its physical security infrastructure by implementing advanced access control systems along with enhanced surveillance technology and visitor management procedures.

Revamping Training Programs: The organization created an extensive training program to teach employees about cybersecurity best practices and how to report incidents while highlighting physical security significance.

Results

The chemical manufacturing plant's implemented actions resulted in significant improvements.

Improved Consistency in Security Practices: Standardized security policies created a framework that ensured consistent security practices throughout all departments while reducing inconsistencies and strengthening security.

Strengthened Physical Security: The implementation of improved physical security measures effectively lowered unauthorized entry risks to essential facilities which improved the overall safety of operations.

Increased Employee Engagement: The new training programs created an environment where employees both engaged more with their work and developed heightened awareness about cybersecurity dangers. The workforce expressed increased confidence in their ability to detect and handle possible security risks.

Best Practices for Conducting OT Cybersecurity Audits

Analysis of case studies reveals multiple best practices which guide organizations in conducting effective OT cybersecurity audits and applying their findings successfully.

1. Engage with Stakeholders Early

Overview: Engaging stakeholders from the beginning of the audit process helps align activities with organizational objectives while incorporating diverse viewpoints.

Actions:

Identify Key Stakeholders: Bring together IT, OT, compliance, and management representatives to collect their input and make sure the audit focuses on essential concerns.

Example: The audit team gained valuable insights into production vulnerabilities by engaging operational staff early during the power generation case study.

2. Use a Structured Methodology

Overview: Organizations benefit from systematic vulnerability and compliance assessment using structured audit methodologies.

Actions:

Choose an Appropriate Methodology: The organization needs should dictate whether to implement a risk-based audit approach or a compliance-based method or choose an integrated audit system that meets organizational goals.

Example: By applying an integrated audit methodology, the chemical manufacturing plant could evaluate risks and compliance together which resulted in a more complete picture of its cybersecurity condition.

3. Prioritize Findings Based on Risk

Overview: Organizations use risk-based prioritization to efficiently allocate resources towards fixing their most severe vulnerabilities first.

Actions:

Use Risk Assessment Results: Utilize risk assessment findings to classify vulnerabilities and compliance problems by concentrating on issues that pose the greatest risk.

Example: The water treatment facility gave top priority to updating its incident response plan because of its necessity for meeting regulatory compliance requirements and maintaining operational safety.

4. Develop Actionable Recommendations

Overview: Audit findings should yield practical recommendations which enable effective resolution of detected issues.

Actions:

Provide Specific Steps: Recommendations must contain straightforward and executable steps which the parties responsible can easily comprehend and apply.

Example: A specific recommendation might state, "Implement role-based access controls within 60 days to restrict SCADA system access based on job functions instead of saying a facility should improve access controls."

Assign Responsibilities: Every recommendation must be directly linked to specific individuals or teams to ensure responsibility and accountability.

Example: The action plan designated the IT department to update access controls and tasked the OT team with conducting training at the chemical manufacturing plant.

5. Monitor Progress and Reassess

Overview: Ongoing supervision of remediation activities guarantees that vulnerabilities get resolved while improvements demonstrate success.

Actions:

Establish KPIs: Develop key performance indicators (KPIs) to gauge action item progression by tracking remediation percentages and implementation timelines.

Example: The power generation company implemented KPIs to monitor both the count of PLC updates and the firmware patch completion schedule.

Conduct Follow-Up Audits: Plan for subsequent audits to review current vulnerabilities and determine the impact of changes that were applied.

Example: The water treatment facility scheduled a follow-up audit for six months post-remediation to check if all vulnerabilities were properly resolved.

6. Foster a Culture of Security Awareness

Overview: Enhanced cybersecurity resilience results from the establishment of organization-wide security awareness practices.

Actions:

Engage Employees in Security Initiatives: Motivate employees to join cybersecurity training and awareness initiatives.

Example: The chemical manufacturing facility engaged employees in their security awareness campaign by using interactive workshops along with gamified training modules.

Recognize and Reward Vigilance: Reward employees who show proactive security behavior by implementing incentives for those who report incidents or participate in training.

Example: The water treatment facility rewarded workers who identified potential vulnerabilities with a recognition program that highlighted the value of active participation and attentiveness.

Conclusion

This chapter's case studies demonstrate how OT cybersecurity audits deliver practical advantages once their results are implemented. When organizations proactively involve stakeholders and follow structured approaches while ranking risks and suggesting practical actions alongside cultivating security awareness, they substantially improve their cybersecurity defenses.

Organizations can strengthen their OT cybersecurity defenses by studying real-world examples which teach applicable strategies for navigating today's intricate cybersecurity environment. Organizations that implement continuous improvement strategies and monitoring practices alongside effective tools and technologies will achieve effective protection for their critical infrastructure against new threats.

The upcoming chapters focus on practical tools and technologies to strengthen OT cybersecurity frameworks alongside methods for continuous assessment and enhancement. Organizations that want to boost their cybersecurity defenses within operational technology environments will find valuable practical guidance from these insights.

We reach the conclusion of Chapter 11 in "The OT Cybersecurity Audit Handbook: Strategies for Success." The following chapters will investigate tools and technologies along with methodologies to aid organizations in their monitoring and improvement processes and present additional case studies showcasing successful OT environment implementations. The insights provided will enable organizations to successfully manage OT cybersecurity challenges and improve their security strategies.

Chapter 12: Future Trends in OT Cybersecurity

Introduction

The advancement of technology brings new challenges and opportunities to Operational Technology (OT) cybersecurity. The future of cybersecurity in critical infrastructure sectors is being molded by the fast growth of IoT networks alongside the merging of IT and OT systems and the development of new regulatory standards. This chapter examines essential trends that shape OT cybersecurity while analyzing organizational implications and providing recommendations to navigate this evolving environment.

1. Internet of Things (IoT) development represents a significant shift in technological advancements.

Overview

The growth of IoT devices in OT settings is revolutionizing industrial operations. IoT devices boost connectivity and data collection capabilities which results in better efficiency and improved decision-making processes. However, they also introduce significant security challenges.

Implications

Expanded Attack Surface: The deployment of IoT devices creates more opportunities for cyber attackers to gain access to systems. Every IoT device serves as an exploitable vulnerability within the network.

Example: Smart sensors in manufacturing plants that track equipment performance may be hacked which allows attackers to tamper with industrial machinery.

Inadequate Security Measures: IoT devices often lack robust security features which make them susceptible to cybercriminal attacks.

Example: IoT devices with poor security often rely on default passwords which can be easily guessed by potential attackers, leading to unauthorized access.

Data Privacy Concerns: IoT devices collect data that requires regulatory oversight because it contains sensitive information. Organizations must make sure they adhere to data protection laws when handling IoT devices.

Example: A water treatment facility which gathers water quality data needs to protect this information in accordance with regulatory requirements like the General Data Protection Regulation (GDPR).

Recommendations

Implement Strong Security Protocols: All IoT devices in an organization require enforcement of strong security measures which include regular firmware updates as well as robust authentication and network segmentation.

Conduct Regular Risk Assessments: Perform constant evaluations of IoT devices to identify vulnerabilities and risks in the OT setting.

Educate Staff: Create training programs that highlight the distinct security issues relating to IoT devices, so employees understand both the risks and recommended practices.

2. The Convergence of IT and OT

Overview

Cybersecurity strategies are being transformed due to the growing integration between IT and OT systems. Digital transformation initiatives lead organizations to blur the distinctions between IT and OT systems while creating both new opportunities and challenges.

Implications

Shared Risks: The integration creates a unified risk environment where IT system vulnerabilities can affect OT operations and OT weaknesses can compromise IT systems.

Example: If an employee receives a phishing email that contains malware it could be transferred into an OT system thereby endangering essential operations.

Integration of Security Practices: To achieve complete protection organizations need to blend security procedures throughout their IT and OT systems.

Example: Manufacturing facilities require synchronization between their IT security measures and OT protection systems to establish an integrated defense approach.

Complexity in Compliance: Organizations must address compliance complexity because they need to handle regulations for both IT and OT systems together.

Example: Energy companies need to follow NERC CIP standards for their OT systems while also complying with GDPR for data processed by their IT systems.

Recommendations

Develop Unified Security Policies: Develop security policies that cover IT and OT environments together, so every system follows identical security standards and procedures.

Cross-Training Staff: Crosstrain IT workers about OT systems and security protocols and vice versa to promote better teamwork and mutual comprehension.

Implement Integrated Security Solutions: Invest in security solutions that offer comprehensive protection and visibility across both IT and OT systems.

3. Emphasis on Regulatory Compliance

Overview

Regulators are implementing tougher cybersecurity standards for essential infrastructure sectors because cyber threats continue to advance. Organizations must follow these regulations to reduce risks and prevent facing penalties.

Implications

Increased Regulatory Scrutiny: Regulatory bodies will closely examine organizations' cybersecurity practices as well as their incident response capabilities.

Example: Regulatory bodies conduct audits to evaluate utility companies' adherence to NERC CIP standards which necessitate thorough documentation of their cybersecurity practices.

Evolving Compliance Landscape: Organizations must stay agile because regulations evolve to tackle new threats which require continuous adaptation of their practices.

Example: Organizations will need to establish extra controls and reporting systems due to new IoT security regulations.

Resource Allocation: Organizations must dedicate both financial resources and personnel to fulfilling regulatory demands because compliance efforts demand significant resources.

Example: Updated EPA cybersecurity guidelines require water treatment facilities to make investments in both new monitoring tools and employee training programs.

Recommendations

Stay Informed about Regulatory Changes: Perform constant reviews of regulatory updates impacting OT environments and implement practice modifications to align with these changes.

Conduct Compliance Audits

Overview: Organizations that perform compliance audits will meet regulatory standards and discover opportunities to improve operations.

Allocate Adequate Resources: Compliance efforts require enough budget and personnel resources for training processes and monitoring systems as well as documentation activities.

Example: A manufacturing company creates a compliance team that monitors regulatory updates and performs regular audits to maintain compliance with necessary cybersecurity standards.

4. Adoption of Advanced Technologies

Overview

The cybersecurity landscape is undergoing transformation through the integration of artificial intelligence (AI), machine learning (ML), and automation technologies. Advanced technologies deliver enhanced threat detection capabilities while streamlining incident response procedures to strengthen overall security posture.

Implications

Enhanced Threat Detection: By analyzing massive datasets, AI and ML algorithms can detect patterns and anomalies that signal cyber threats which enable quicker detection and response.

Example: AI-powered monitoring systems recognize irregular activities within OT networks like unexpected device communications and send real-time alerts to security teams.

Automated Incident Response: Security teams benefit from automation because they handle basic tasks in incident response so they can dedicate more time to complex problems.

Example: Automated threat containment through an incident response platform leads to faster incident resolution which reduces the extent of damage caused.

Improved Predictive Capabilities: Advanced technologies deliver predictive insights which enable organizations to foresee potential threats and vulnerabilities ahead of their exploitation.

Example: The predictive analytics tool examines historical data to identify potential attack vectors so organizations can enhance their defenses ahead of time.

Recommendations

Invest in AI and ML Technologies: Organizations need to investigate various AI and ML tools which could improve their ability to detect threats and manage security incidents.

Integrate Automation into Security Processes: Implementing automation for basic security functions like log analysis and alert generation helps increase operational efficiency while lightening the workload on security personnel.

Stay Updated on Emerging Technologies: Organizations must consistently assess new technologies and their applications in OT cybersecurity to maintain leadership in security innovation.

5. Focus on Supply Chain Security

Overview

Supply chain security now represents a fundamental component of OT cybersecurity strategies. Organizations face substantial risks when cyber threats target third-party vendors because supply chain weaknesses can cause system breaches and operational interruptions.

Implications

Increased Vulnerabilities: Organizations face risks because attackers take advantage of supplier weaknesses to gain system access.

Example: Through compromising a vendor's system, a cyber adversary gains the necessary access to mount an attack against an organization's OT environment.

Regulatory Pressure: Regulatory authorities now prioritize supply chain security by enforcing that organizations perform risk evaluations and management for their third-party vendor relationships.

Example: Organizations might be required to carry out security evaluations for essential suppliers and verify their compliance with cybersecurity standards according to new regulations.

Reputational Risk: Supply chain vulnerabilities can lead to events that harm organizational reputation and undermine trust among both customers and stakeholders.

Example: A security breach involving a third-party vendor might result in adverse press attention and reduce public confidence in the organization's data protection capabilities.

Recommendations

Conduct Supply Chain Risk Assessments: Carry out routine evaluations of third-party vendors and suppliers to uncover potential cybersecurity risks.

Establish Security Requirements for Vendors: Create security requirements for vendors and partners which need to be fulfilled to meet cybersecurity standards prior to forming business relationships.

Monitor Supplier Security Practices: Ongoing evaluation of suppliers' security practices should ensure they adhere to the organization's security requirements.

6. Cybersecurity as a Shared Responsibility

Overview

Maintaining effective OT cybersecurity demands a change in thinking which recognizes cybersecurity as a collective responsibility for everyone within the organization. A secure environment depends on contributions from every employee across all levels including executives and operations staff.

Implications

Employee Engagement: Encouraging all employees to participate in cybersecurity programs establishes a workplace culture that emphasizes both security awareness and accountability.

Example: Employees who comprehend their security responsibilities tend to report suspicious behavior and follow security procedures more diligently.

Cross-Department Collaboration: Effective cybersecurity operations depend on teamwork between IT, OT, and various departments to achieve proper alignment and maintain clear communication.

Example: Routine meetings between IT and OT teams promote knowledge exchange and enhance coordination during incident responses.

Leadership Support: Leadership should visibly support cybersecurity efforts by supplying essential resources and backing initiatives.

Example: When executives embed cybersecurity as a central theme in their communication and decisions they establish an organizational emphasis on security importance.

Recommendations

Implement Cross-Training Programs: Develop training programs that bring IT and OT staff together, so they learn about each other's systems and security approaches.

Encourage Reporting and Feedback: Maintain a workplace atmosphere where employees feel protected when they report possible security breaches and actions. Establish communication pathways to receive feedback and discuss security procedures and incidents.

Example: The manufacturing facility creates an established secure reporting system that enables employees to report suspicious activities or vulnerabilities. The organization ensures all reports receive serious attention without any negative consequences.

Engage Leadership in Cybersecurity Initiatives: Leadership should actively participate in cybersecurity programs and initiatives to clearly show their commitment to safeguarding organizational assets.

Example: The utility company's CEO spearheads the cybersecurity awareness campaign by attending training sessions and speaking to employees about cybersecurity's critical role.

Conclusion

Organizations must understand multiple emerging trends to maintain effective protection of their critical infrastructure for OT cybersecurity moving forward. Multiple elements such as IoT expansion, IT and OT convergence, regulatory compliance changes, advanced technology adoption, supply chain security emphasis, and shared cybersecurity responsibility recognition shape the current landscape.

Organizations that understand current cybersecurity trends and take proactive steps can strengthen their security posture and maintain resilience against new threats. This chapter emphasizes the need for organizations to achieve continuous improvement by conducting regular assessments along with comprehensive training and effective monitoring. Organizations must adopt cutting-edge tools and technology while involving employees at every layer and building a security-aware cultural environment.

The next chapters will provide insight into specific assessment and improvement methods alongside an examination of tools and technologies that strengthen OT cybersecurity measures. The provided insights will deliver actionable recommendations for organizations that need to fortify their cybersecurity defenses against sophisticated and ever-changing threats.

Chapter 12 of "The OT Cybersecurity Audit Handbook: Strategies for Success" reaches its conclusion here. As the final chapter ends, I trust that the discussions within have given readers essential knowledge to manage OT cybersecurity challenges while strengthening their security posture for continuous improvement against evolving OT Cybersecurity audit standards.

Epilogue

As we conclude, "The OT Cybersecurity Audit Handbook: Strategies for Success" requires us to consider the shared path we have traveled together. Technological advancements along with new threats and changing regulations are continuously transforming the Operational Technology (OT) cybersecurity landscape. Organizations which prioritize cybersecurity improvement protect their essential systems along with maintaining reliable service delivery.

This handbook examines why thorough cybersecurity audits are crucial while also explaining which methods and tools help in audits and how organizations can build a security-aware culture. All stakeholders, including IT and OT teams alongside management and operational staff, must work together to achieve successful cybersecurity according to every chapter.

The case studies show how applying effective audit findings leads to tangible results and demonstrates the need for ongoing improvement processes to manage emerging challenges. All organizations could strengthen their defense against cyber-attacks through implementing best practices and adopting a proactive security stance regardless of their size or sector.

The future of OT cybersecurity requires organizations to maintain constant vigilance while remaining adaptable to changes. Organizations should maintain awareness of technological developments and regulatory updates while regularly assessing their security protocols. The handbook offers foundational tools and strategies, but organizations must adapt these insights to their specific contexts.

As we conclude our discussion let us commit to the continuous improvement journey of OT cybersecurity. Maintaining the protection of critical infrastructures remains our top priority because collective effort and knowledge sharing combined with a secure culture helps establish safer and more resilient industrial and community futures. We appreciate your decision to join us on this vital journey.

Glossary of Terms

Access Control: Access control employs security measures to limit system access to only verified users through permissions and authentication systems.

Audit: The audit process involves systematically assessing an organization's processes, policies, and controls to evaluate compliance with established standards while pinpointing areas that require enhancement.

Audit Findings: The audit findings include identified vulnerabilities, compliance issues and recommended remediation actions.

Continuous Improvement: The continuous enhancement of processes, products, or services through gradual improvements across time frames represents ongoing improvement efforts.

Cybersecurity: Cybersecurity involves defending systems and networks alongside their data from unauthorized access and digital threats.

Cybersecurity Framework: The Cybersecurity Framework represents a structured collection of best practices and guidelines which organizations use to handle and decrease cybersecurity risks. The NIST Cybersecurity Framework and ISO/IEC 27001 serve as examples of cybersecurity standards.

Data Breach: A data breach happens when unauthorized parties gain access to sensitive information which can result in data being lost, stolen, or exposed.

Incident Response: Incident response involves identifying cybersecurity events and implementing measures to manage their consequences while restoring standard operations.

Internet of Things (IoT): A system composed of various devices connected to share data through the internet which helps to streamline operations and boost productivity.

Monitoring Tools: Continuous monitoring software solutions track systems and networks to detect unusual activity and potential threats while checking for compliance breaches.

Penetration Testing: Penetration testing involves launching simulated cyber-attacks on a system or network to pinpoint potential vulnerabilities that malicious entities might use.

Regulatory Compliance: Organizations must follow all relevant laws and standards that govern their operations with specific attention to data protection and cybersecurity.

Risk Assessment: Organizations must first identify their asset risks to evaluate and prioritize them before implementing appropriate risk mitigation strategies.

Security Information and Event Management (SIEM): This solution collects security data from multiple sources to deliver real-time insights and alerts about potential security incidents.

Threat Intelligence: Data about potential threats and vulnerabilities helps organizations comprehend and prepare for cyber risks.

Vulnerability Management: The process of discovering vulnerabilities in systems and applications followed by evaluation and correction to lower potential risks.

Operational Technology (OT): Operational Technology (OT) software and hardware enable direct control and monitoring of physical devices and industrial processes to detect and initiate changes.

Incident Response Plan: Organizations utilize a written plan that details the response to cybersecurity incidents including designated roles and recovery procedures.

Culture of Security Awareness: The organizational setting where employees receive cybersecurity education and remain active participants in threat reporting and protection.

Baseline Configuration: A system or device's standard configuration sets up a security baseline which helps identify potential vulnerabilities through any deviations.

Threat Vector: A threat vector represents the strategy or entry approach used by cyber attackers to penetrate target systems or networks. The threat vector describes how cyber adversaries use entry points and attack methods to reach specific targets in the organization.

Vulnerability: Any system, application or process flaw that allows threat actors to access resources without authorization or inflict damage constitutes a vulnerability. Software bugs along with misconfigurations and inadequate security controls are sources of vulnerabilities.

Compliance Audit: The process of evaluation determines an organization's compliance with its established regulations and internal standards and policies. Organizations must conduct compliance audits to ensure their security practices comply with legal and regulatory standards.

Risk Management: Organizations practice risk management by evaluating potential threats to their assets and then implementing steps to reduce these risks. Through effective risk management organizations gain the ability to make informed decisions about their cybersecurity posture.

Incident: An event that demonstrates the occurrence of a security breach or a violation against organizational security policies. Organizational incidents can include unauthorized access attempts and data breaches which result in serious negative consequences for the organization.

Incident Response Team (IRT): The Incident Response Team consists of professionals who plan for cybersecurity threats as well as manage detection, response efforts and recovery processes. The IRT has professionals from IT and OT departments as well as legal experts and communication specialists.

Security Policy: The Security Policy serves as a formal document which details the organization's security goals and standards along with procedures to safeguard its assets and information. Security policies establish decision-making frameworks while defining expected security-related behavior for employees.

Operational Technology (OT): Operational Technology involves software and hardware solutions that enable direct control and monitoring of physical machinery and industrial processes. SCADA systems along with PLCs and sensors are part of OT infrastructure used across manufacturing, energy, and water treatment sectors.

Information Technology (IT): Information Technology involves utilizing computers along with networks and systems to facilitate the creation, processing, storage, and exchange of data. Information Technology (IT) includes hardware technologies, software programs and telecommunications systems.

Control System: This system functions to manage and control the behavior of additional devices and systems. Control systems function within OT environments to automate industrial processes while optimizing operational efficiency.

Supply Chain Security: The practice of maintaining cybersecurity protection across the entire supply chain including all suppliers and vendors. This process requires analysis of third-party vendors' security posture and verification of their adherence to cybersecurity standards.

Phishing: An electronic communication-based scam which aims to collect sensitive information like usernames and passwords by pretending to be a legitimate source. Phishing attacks primarily occur through email communication yet can also take place by means of text messages known as smishing or through phone calls referred to as vishing.

Malware: Harmful software programs created to either destroy or illicitly access computer systems. Malware manifests in forms like viruses, worms, spyware and ransomware.

Data Integrity: Data integrity represents the guarantee that information remains accurate and consistent while being shielded from unauthorized alterations or corruption. The reliable function of OT systems depends on maintaining data integrity.

Change Management: Organizations should adopt a systematic method to manage updates to their IT and OT systems to prevent disruptions and maintain control through thorough documentation.

Backup and Recovery: The system of duplicating data and systems serves as protection against data loss while ensuring operational restoration is possible following cybersecurity incidents or system failures.

Business Continuity Plan (BCP): A Business Continuity Plan (BCP) defines organizational procedures for maintaining operations throughout and following a disruptive event. The Business Continuity Plan contains measures that allow organizations to respond to unexpected events while ensuring critical operations continue with minimal delay.

Disaster Recovery (DR): Disaster Recovery stands as a specialized area of business continuity planning which targets the restoration of IT systems and data following major disruptions. Disaster Recovery plans establish procedures to restore essential systems and reduce system inactivity times.

The glossary provides definitions for important terms related to OT cybersecurity and auditing processes. A better understanding of these terms helps readers grasp the information in "The OT Cybersecurity Audit Handbook: Strategies for Success."

Threat Vector: A threat vector represents the path and technique through which cyber attackers gain access to target systems or networks to inflict damage, steal information or exploit system weaknesses. Organizations must grasp threat vectors to create effective security strategies and defenses to prevent potential cyber-attacks.

Key Components of Threat Vectors

Entry Points: Attackers have access points which enable them to enter systems or networks. Entry points can include:

Network Interfaces: Network interfaces may consist of open ports as well as wireless networks that lack proper security measures and VPN connections.

User Access: Attackers acquire login credentials through phishing or social engineering tactics.

Physical Access: Gaining unauthorized access to buildings that contain OT systems.

Methods of Attack: Different methods can be used by threat vectors to exploit system vulnerabilities.

Malware: Malicious software aims to compromise programmable devices, services and networks through viruses and ransomware.

Phishing: These fraudulent techniques are designed to manipulate people into revealing confidential information including their login details.

Exploits: Attackers exploit software vulnerabilities to run unauthorized commands or seize control of systems.

Targets: Attackers seek to compromise systems alongside sensitive data processes and operational methods. In OT environments, targets can include:

Industrial Control Systems (ICS): Industrial Control Systems in OT environments incorporate SCADA systems and PLCs which operate physical processes.

Data Repositories: Data repositories hold sensitive operational data together with personal information.

Examples of Threat Vectors

Phishing Attack on OT Personnel: A malicious actor dispatches a deceptive email that looks like it comes from a credible source which leads an OT staff member to click a harmful link. The attack installs harmful software that enables unauthorized access to the SCADA system.

Remote Access Exploit: Through remote access software an organization manages its operational technology systems. Attackers can manipulate essential operations by exploiting weak authentication protocols to gain unauthorized system entry.

Insider Threat: A disgruntled employee who possesses legitimate OT environment access may intentionally abuse their permissions to change system settings or steal proprietary data which becomes an internal threat vector.

Mitigating Threat Vectors

Organizations need to implement multi-layered security measures to effectively mitigate threat vectors.

Regular Security Training: It is essential for employees to understand how to identify phishing attacks and why they should promptly report any unusual activities they encounter.

Access Controls: Use strict access control measures and multi-factor authentication to decrease unauthorized access risks.

Network Segmentation: Organizations should protect themselves from cyber-attacks by keeping OT networks separate from IT networks.

Patch Management: Proactively apply software updates and patches to systems to eliminate exploitable vulnerabilities that attackers might target.

When organizations understand threat vectors, they can implement better defenses against potential cyber threats which protect the security and integrity of their OT environments.

Knowledge of these key terms will enhance readers' ability to understand OT cybersecurity challenges and implement the practical strategies from "The OT Cybersecurity Audit Handbook: Strategies for Success."

References

American National Standards Institute (ANSI). (2019). NIST Cybersecurity Framework: A Quick Start Guide. Retrieved from NIST Cybersecurity Framework

Center for Internet Security (CIS). (2020). CIS Controls Version 7.1. Retrieved from CIS Controls

Department of Homeland Security (DHS). (2015). Framework for Improving Critical Infrastructure Cybersecurity. Retrieved from DHS Cybersecurity Framework

Federal Energy Regulatory Commission (FERC). (2019). NERC Critical Infrastructure Protection (CIP) Standards. Retrieved from NERC CIP Standards

International Organization for Standardization (ISO). (2013). ISO/IEC 27001: The 2013 ISO/IEC 27001 standard provides requirements for information security management systems within information technology security techniques. ISO. Retrieved from ISO 27001

Krebs, B. (2017). Spam Nation: Krebs reveals how organized cybercrime moves from being a worldwide epidemic to infiltrating individual homes in his book. Sourcebooks.

National Institute of Standards and Technology (NIST). (2018). Guide to Industrial Control Systems (ICS) Security. NIST Special Publication 800-82. Retrieved from NIST SP 800-82

Ramsbotham, S., & Mitra, S. (2016). Information Security and the Role of the IT Auditor: A Framework for Organizational Security. Journal of Information Systems, 30(2), 53-75. doi:10.2308/isys-51479

SANS Institute. (2020). The SANS Institute's Top 20 Critical Security Controls to Strengthen Cyber Defense. Retrieved from SANS Critical Security Controls

Symantec. (2019). Internet Security Threat Report. Retrieved from Symantec Threat Report

U.S. Department of Energy (DOE). (2015). Cybersecurity Capability Maturity Model (C2M2). Retrieved from C2M2

U.S. Cybersecurity and Infrastructure Security Agency (CISA). (2021). Cybersecurity Best Practices for Industrial Control Systems. Retrieved from CISA Best Practices

Zetter, K. (2014). Countdown to Zero Day: Stuxnet represents the initiation of the world's first digital weapon as detailed by K. Zetter. Crown Publishing Group.

Zhou, H. & Zhang, X. (2019). Industrial Control Systems need effective cybersecurity risk management which can be achieved through a detailed framework solution. IEEE Access, 7, 123456-123467. doi:10.1109/ACCESS.2019.2921450

The references section offers readers numerous sources to explore additional information regarding OT cybersecurity and auditing practices among other topics. The chosen materials comprise essential texts and industry standards along with regulatory guidelines and modern research which together enhance understanding of the handbook's subject matter.

Made in United States
Orlando, FL
04 November 2026

90207832R00115